Grace Restored

Reignite your Love, Faith, Hope & Zeal for Christ

Grace Restored

Reignite your Love, Faith, Hope & Zeal for Christ

Ramos Talaya

For more info:
www.ramostalaya.blogspot.com
www.linkedin.com/in/ramostalaya
www.facebook.com/psRamosTalaya
www.twitter.com/RamosTalaya
www.youtube.com/user/RamosTalaya
www.google.com/+RamosTalaya
www.instagram.com/Ramos_Talaya

ISBN:
Softcover: 978-0-620-92943-1
eBook: 978-0-620-92944-8
Audio Book: 978-0-620-92945-5

Contents

Dedicated to God our Father, who gave His only begotten
Son to die for our sins, so that we may live.
And to our Lord Jesus Christ, the Son of the Father, who out
of pure love, laid down His life that He may wash us in His
precious blood, and present us faultless before the throne of
the Majesty on High.

And to the Holy Spirit, the Creator and Giver of life, who
revealed the holiness of God to our exceeding sinful souls. He
showed us our wretched hearts, convicted us of our sins,
brought us to our knees, gave us grace to repent, regenerated
our souls, and translated us unto the Kingdom of the dear
Son of God.

O LORD our God, the Triune God, the Father, the Son and
the Holy Spirit, the God to whom all praise, worship and
adoration belongs, take Your glory! For every Spirit-inspired
deed, done in loving obedience, take Your glory; for we offer
it all in the name of Christ Jesus our Lord, through the power
of the Holy Spirit, for Your glory alone, Amen!

To God

O God, Ocean of Love! Who can phantom the abyss of Your love for Adam's lost race? Who can ascend to the unapproachable light, tell us the height of Your mercy, and the width of Your grace for us poor sinners?

Oh, "Blessed hand that drew the plan of salvation!"

Who can reconcile Your irreconcilable hatred for sin, with *"It pleased the LORD to bruise Him"*—Him, the spotless and blameless Son of Your love? Whom You gave over to the wrath of Your justice, so that You may lift up the sceptre of Your mercy to the repentant and returning sinner and take him upon Your arms of love?

Shall we, who are saved at such incalculable cost to Yourself, once again be friends with Your enemy, that old serpent, the devil; and mock You with our pretence love, while we wallow in our sins? God forbid!

Father of Christ Jesus, take Your glory!

In every sin we overcome by Your grace, take Your glory.

In every good deed we do by Your grace, take Your glory.

You are worthy oh LORD, of our prayers, praises, worship, reverence, and obedience. Take Your glory!

O Spotless Lamb of God! You who suffered excruciating pain and agony for my exceeding sinful soul, and washed me in Your precious blood; what can I say to You?

Oh, to think of You carrying that heavy cross on Your back, for a wretch like me; how can my heart not be moved to love You enough to hate sin?

What a joy divine when I first believed and received the pardon of my sins! But alas Master, my forgiveness cost You everything, even Your own life!

When with the eyes of faith, my soul gazes upon You, I need no other arguments to love You. The five wound scars, yet visible on Your glorified body, is sufficient. Master, You have won my heart, body and soul. Please give me grace to love You more and more!

You are worthy, O Christ, to "Receive the reward of Your sufferings." For you were slain, and bought me with Your precious blood; therefore, I am whole Yours, now and through all eternity. Be glorified in my life, O Son of God!

O Immaculate Spirit! Beautiful, majestic and altogether glorious!

O Blessed Holy Spirit! You who proceed from the Father and the Son, and together with the Father and the Son, are One God. Worthy to be praised, revered and worshiped, what a wonder You are!

When You opened my eyes and revealed the holiness of God to my wretched soul, it was a mystery divine. You exposed my exceeding sinful heart, and convicted me of my vile sins, iniquities and transgressions in the light of God. You brought me down on my knees in bitter tears, let me stew under severe conviction, pangs, and anguish. You helped me to travail for my soul. And blessed be God, for that blessed hour, when in despair over my sins, You, O Blessed Spirit, pointed me to the Crucified Son of God, and gave me grace to repent and believe on Christ Jesus, my God! Oh, blessed be the God and Father of my Saviour Jesus Christ, who pitied me, a wretched sinner, and granted me repentance, and pardon all my grievous sins for the sake of the Lamb slain for me, even me! And through His Spirit, translated me into the Kingdom of His Dear Son. Oh, Praise the LORD oh my soul, and forget not His love, mercy and grace; and worship and serve Him, and Him only; who created you, redeemed you and adopted you to an incorruptible inheritance in Christ Jesus, your God, Amen.

O Triune God, Triune God, Triune God. How glorious is the beauty and fragrance of Your Holiness!

How boundless and bundling is the gulf of Your pure love!

How lovely and beautiful are Your ways; how truthful and faithful You are!

Who can tell and measure the wonder of Your wisdom, oh, Majesty Divine!

LORD God Almighty! Who can withstand and resist the strength of Your might power?

Glory be to You, oh the Most High God, for You created all things, and by Your will all things exist and were created to the praise and the honor of Your Glory!

I love You, O LORD! There is none like You.

I am Yours!

You created me, therefore, You are my God. Thank you for giving me a being.

You redeemed me, therefore, You are my Master. Thank you for giving me Life.

You have adopted me, therefore, You are my Father.

Thank You for making me Your co-heir with Christ.

My God, Master and Father, take Your Glory, in Christ Jesus my Saviour, Amen.

I am very grateful to the Holy Spirit
and all the ministers of the gospel of Truth who were used by God to
help me shape this book.

To all my physical and spiritual family,
I'm very grateful for your support.
It would be impossible without you.

To all pilgrims and my companions in the Lord
in this spiritual journey of life unto eternal life,
thank you for your love, prayers, wisdom,
caring,
and support in times of need.
May God repay you a hundredfold. In Jesus' name.
Amen!

A Journey Back to God

"The heart is deceitful above all things, and desperately wicked; who can know it?" -Jeremiah 17:9

Oh, who can describe in detail, the indescribable pain, sorrow of heart, grief of spirit and mourning of the believing soul that is genuinely born again of the Spirit of God, and loves Christ Jesus in sincerity, after fallen into sin again?

Oh, with what moans, heavy sighs and groans the redeemed soul laments for crucifying the Son of God afresh and grieving the Spirit of grace?

Anyone who has ever broken a bone, will testify of the excruciating pain of cracked bones! And anyone who loves God (with the exception of the "Perfect Christian,") will relate with a heavy sigh, the dark nights our souls go through, when our own sins and rebellion against God, separate us from Him, Who alone is Light. David calls the separation, "Broken bones," and Job says, "It is heavier than the sand on the seashore."

In despair, we go forward, He is not there. We go backwards, He is not there either. We turn sideways, and there is no sense of Him or His presence. Oh, the dreadful night of the soul!

In despondency, our dejected soul is prone to cry out, "I am cut off from my God!"

Nothing can quiet the turmoil inside the redeemed soul that has fallen into sin. Our loved ones, friends, pastors, teachers and the like, are in this case all "Miserable comforters." Though they mean well, their word of comfort is like a bucket that cannot reach the water in the well, to a parched man.

Without forgiveness, our souls will forever roam around this sad world, hopeless and down cast, until one day the grave calls our name, and in misery and fear we depart from this evil world. Yet we do not need to suffer this fate. The Spirit of Christ can restore the joy of our salvation, when he sends His Holy Spirit to your soul saying, "Your sins are forgiven."

This book is a humble attempt to aid God's children to avoid such tragic end—to die in ones' sins.

The Journey

This is a very short book. It comprises only twelve chapters.

In order to gain what this book offers, you are required to set aside twelve days of your life and wholly devote them to restore your relationship with God through Christ, by the Holy Spirit.

What this means, is that the One offended, is a Holy God. Any casual dealings and attitudes will not suffice. It will require a solemn approach to God, a repentant spirit, a setting of the heart, and willingness of the mind to clean up our act and make things right with God; with a holy determination, not only to obtain mercy and forgiveness for our sins, but also to plead for God's grace to go and sin no more. Anything less than that, mocks the Great God of Heaven, who knows everything and knows more about us than we know about ourselves.

For the next twelve days, refrain from anything that distracts and entertains you. Except for your necessary duties (work, study or business), cut off everything else: TV, movies, going out, social media,

Whatsapp, or other distracting phone apps. Texting apps will probably be one of the biggest challenges, but you can still use it when necessary, such as work, study, business and family communications. All other chitchat must be utterly cut off. If it is your source of employment, required for school, or family to use one of these items proceed, otherwise limit your use.

If married, talk to your spouse and come into an agreement. However, if your spouse disagrees, please fulfil your marital duties, without holding any grudges, or labelling your spouse uncaring. This is your personal Journey. Fulfilling your non-consenting spouse's marital needs will not affect you from obtaining the end result of this journey.

I suggest you only read one chapter a day, and that you invite the Lord Jesus to be your partner during the twelve days' journey. After reading each day, you must have a discussion with the Lord Jesus Christ about the challenges you are facing in implementing these truths into your life, where you are falling short, and ask for His help and the Holy Spirit's guidance. Be honest, God knows all. There is no point in pretending before Him. Your honesty and sincerity towards God determine how you grow spiritually.

At the close of each day, there are meditation time guidelines, which comprises of Scripture reading, memory precepts, and commitment to obey the precepts; memory promise, have faith on the promise, and heart talks.

Meditation Time: Sin has not just affected our souls and bodies, but also our faculties. Our minds struggle to focus for a long time, and our memory fails to remember everything. Meditation is God's gracious remedy to help us focus on what really matters and reminds us of the things that are essential.

Unless you meditate on what you read each day, you will most likely not retain what you have read, and perhaps at most, remember very little of the things that really matter. Meditation is to fix our mind on a particular subject/object until, by the grace of God, the subject/object begins to expound and unravel itself to our better understanding.

Precept: Precepts are God's road signs to prevent us from falling into the pitfalls of this fallen world. Everyone that desires to reach his God-ordained destination, must learn and endeavour to follow closely the road signs God has placed on the way that leads us to our destination.

Commitment to obey God's Precepts: Many Christians live defeated and shallow lives, because of the unwillingness to commit to obey God's precepts. God always provides His grace to those who are willing and committed to do as He commands. Please make commitments to obey God's precepts, and then, by God's grace, stick to them.

Promises: Promises are God's highways that lead us to the treasures of heaven. Everything we need are locked inside God's treasure coffer, and God's promises are the only keys that unlock His coffer. Praying without a promise is presumption. The promises are the roads, and the precepts are the road signs. And he who carefully follows the road and closely obeys the signs, increases the chance of reaching his destination.

Having Faith on the Promise: God keeps his Covenant, Amen. God doesn't owe us anything, yet out of the goodness of His heart, He provided great and precious promises, and bound Himself to fulfil ALL His promises, without fail, to all who obey His precepts.
Promises are checks given to us by God. A check remains just a piece of paper, until the bearer cashes it out. The promises are our inheritance; unless we maintain them by faith, and plead them before the throne of grace, they will remain unclaimed. Therefore, we must not only believe

the promises of God, but also, with all reverence, we must by faith press them before God until we receive what God has promised.

Heart-talk: We were created with an inborn need to have a vital relationship with God. Without it, Christianity becomes nothing more than a sterile system of do's and don'ts. I believe, one of the main reasons so many good Christians fail to enjoy a satisfying relationship with God, is the lack of sincerity, and that unavailing self-imposed pretence. By lack of sincerity and self-imposed pretence, I hereby don't mean hypocrisy. A hypocrite can never have a relationship with God. I mean that guile art we have learned from our fallen nature; the ability to sift in our minds, speak in prayer what we deem as acceptable to God, and leave our true feelings unuttered. Surely, we ought to fear God, and regard Him with utmost reverence. No child of God will cast away his fear and reverence for God while being sincere and guileless before Him. On the contrary, it is fear and reverence that should prompt us to acknowledge God as Omniscient, encouraging us to candidly pour our heart before Him.

Since we know and believe that God knows everything, and hears the thoughts of our heart, why then pretend before Him? Unless we become like little children and tell our Heavenly Father, our pain, distresses, confusions, failures, godly desires and learn to express our true feelings, we will never experience God the way we are meant to. Therefore, at the end of each meditation time, there is space allocated for you to reverently and sincerely, pour your heart to God. Dare be honest with Him, and He will speak to you plainly.

Prayer: Prayer is the key the Holy Spirit uses to unlock the mysteries of the Kingdom of God and reveal the things freely given to us.
At the end of each chapter, you will find a prayer to help you start. Feel free to expound these prayers by adding words of your own, as the Spirit leads.

Refrain from using these prayers in any public or group settings; these prayers are meant for God's ears only.

Prayer Guidelines:

1st prayer 5:30am
2nd prayer Anytime between 12:00pm– 3:00pm
3rd prayer Anytime between 6:00pm – 10:00pm

Daily Scripture Reading: The Word of God is the spiritual seed that the Holy Spirit planted in our dead hearts. The Word is the living waters He used to irrigate the planted seed and allow the life of Christ to germinate in our souls. Thus we are born again. However, sin and rebellion against God, brings death to our soul and allows the life of Christ in our souls to wither away. The only way to revive it, is to water our dry hearts, and make our souls wet with the dew of the Word of God, until the life of Christ revives within us. This is what daily Scripture readings are for.
Some prefer daily Bible reading before praying, while others prefer praying first. I suggest you use the method that works best for you.

If you currently have a daily Bible reading system, do not disrupt it, simply add these to your daily readings.

Memory Precepts and Promise: Each day comes with a precept and a promise that summarizes and reinforces the topic of the day. I suggest you write the precept and the promise in a small piece of paper and stick it someplace visible while you work, study, or conduct business. Create a habit, each time your eyes are directed to the precepts, make a thought prayer in your heart concerning them or anything else as your heart is prompted.

Leaning on Christ: In John fifteen, verse five, Christ says, *"I am the vine, you are the branches. He who abides in Me, and I in him, bears much fruit;*

for without Me you can do nothing" (John 15:5). All the above principles will be difficult to implement unless Christ extends you His helping hand. Exercise self-discipline and ask the Lord Jesus to accompany you. Ask for His grace in every prayer and Scripture reading, so you are able to understand the teachings of each day.

Before you sleep, in your evening prayer, ask, "Lord Jesus, please wake me tomorrow early in the morning to pray, and please help me to pray prayers in the Holy Spirit."

In the morning, after He wakes you up, before leaving your bed, lift your heart to God and pray, "Thank You for waking me and thank You for keeping my soul in the land of the living. This is the day You have created, please give me grace to rejoice in it. Please order my steps so all that I do, say, or think may bring glory to Your holy name. Father, please give me grace to pray, and please help me to fix my mind on You while I pray. I ask all these in the name of Jesus, Amen."

When you kneel down to pray (if it's possible for you to kneel), pray, "Lord please give me the spirit of prayer and help me to pray. Please give me grace to be silent when You want to speak to me and the grace to hear Your voice while I kneel in silence before You."

Before doing your daily Scripture reading, kneel before God, holding your Bible, then pray, "Father as I prepare to read and study Your Word, please accompany me and bless me abundantly with wisdom, knowledge, and understanding. Guide me to understand Your Word and apply it to my own personal salvation. Help me respond to questions from those who seek answers and lead them unto their own personal salvation. Grant me the ability to share Your Word with others, with the power and authority given to us by our Lord Jesus Christ, Amen."

The above prayers are only guidelines and you can put them in your own words.

This is a sacrificial journey. You are required to get out of your comfort zone!

- You must pray at least 3 times a day.

- You must learn to have heart-talks with God.

- You must make commitments, and by God's grace, stick to them.

> *"But those who wait on the LORD shall renew their strength . . ."*
> *(Isaiah 40:31).*

See you in the loving arms of God our Father, by the blood of Jesus Christ our Lord. Amen!

Ramos Talaya

I

Returning to the Father

"I will arise and go to my father, and will say to him, "Father, I have sinned against heaven and before you.".Luke 15:18

There comes a time in our lives, when we reach the staggering realization, that there is no life or joy outside of Christ. Whether through lack of joy and meaning or through the painful consequences of our rebellion against God, we all, at some point, come to ourselves and ponder at our idiocy.

A time when our conscience frowns at us, and our heart condemns and reproaches us for our folly.

The sin that, seemed, desirous, delicious, attractive, beautiful, and promised pleasure, has now turned loathsome, distasteful, ugly, and bitter. The sugarcoating wore off, and the deceitful dressing now appears in its true garment and color. We see with dread what a monster sin really is.

Then, we realize it is the same old master, who has enslaved us our entire lives, and together with satan, ruled over us with rigor. Until, in despair, we called out to God to deliver us. Christ set us free from the bondage of sin and satan. By His Cross, Christ broke the yoke of these two tyrants and oppressors, and set us free. Here we arrive again, back in the arms of these two oppressors. Our backs now turned on the meek Son of God, we crucify and shame Him afresh. Allowing the devil, the flesh, and sin an occasion to blaspheme and mock God!

The sin which promised us so much pleasure and happiness, has only brought us spiritual death, sadness, hopelessness, and great shame.

Now, ashamed we look at ourselves with loathing, astonished at what we are capable of. When we reject the counsel of God, and in rebellion insist on our own ways, we will always and without fail feel guilty, shameful, disgusted, and joyless. Even worse, we are always left to pick up the pieces of our lives - shattered by sin - alone. Neither the devil, nor the flesh, nor even our partners in crime will stick around to help us pick up the pieces. They all forsake and abandon us! They display their true colors and prove they are not our friends, but rather enemies of our souls. We must learn to address our enemies properly if we want victory over them.

At this junction of your life, you are confronted with three choices:

i. **Live a purposeless,** useless, joyless and hopeless sin-confess "Christian life," until the grave calls your name, and you cross to the other side of eternity. There God awaits you with a frown on His face to pronounce your eternal destination.

ii. **Be proud,** and recklessly continue to live your life in open rebellion against God while loving your sins more than loving God. Ultimately, you die in your sins and God sends you where you belong, spending eternity in hell, with the devil and everyone and everything that is sinful.

iii. **Or you can truly repent of ALL your sins,** turn to God with ALL your heart, and plead for mercy through the precious blood of Christ Jesus our Lord, and beg for restoration. And declare an irreconcilable war against all the enemies of your soul—the devil, the flesh, sin and the world. And by the grace of God, live a life loving, trusting, and obeying God. Which is the recipe of a fruitful, joyful, purposeful and Spirt-filled life.

These are the three choices available in this fallen world. Anything else is self-deception and illusion.

If you chose one of the first two options, you can stop reading the book here, it will only be a grievous waste of your time, and I would like to spare you of that.

If you have chosen the third option, please hold my hand, my dear beloved, and let's walk through this journey together.

Blessed be the LORD God, our Father, for He is Omniscient Divine, Amen! God in His infinite foreknowledge, foresaw that we, His weak, helpless and pitiful children, born of flesh, and who carry this heavy and deceitful body of death with us, would be prone to fall into sin. In His infinite wisdom, the Merciful God made provision for the retuning of His prodigal children. He placed stepping-stones in His Word, to guide us into a repentance that is acceptable and pleasing to Him, so that He may freely forgive us and restore the joy of His salvation in our souls, through Christ Jesus our Lord, by His Holy Spirit, Amen!

Here are five stepping-stones we can deduct from the Word of God, of what constitutes a genuine repentance that pleases and glorifies our God and Father in heaven:

i. **Holy Resolution to Return to the Father:** "*I will arise and go to my Father,*" Luke 15:18. Feeling guilty and disgusted with ourselves is not enough. We need a holy resolution in our souls, and a solemn determination in our hearts, and a sincere commitment in our will to hate any notion that makes us amiable to any sin; a holy resolution to repent from our sins, a fierce declaration of war against every sin in our lives, and an acute desire to return wholehearted to our Father. Not just to be forgiven, but also with a determined conscious decision, by grace of God, to love, trust, obey, and joyfully serve Him, as long as we live.

In returning to God, we must take sides with Him against ourselves and our sins. We must make no attempts whatsoever, to justify, defend, or make any excuses. We shall not transfer the blame to the devil, sinning partners, or circumstances. We must accept our sins, take full responsibility for them, and totally agree with God's displeasure and hatred for our sins.

ii. **Godly Sorrow:** *"For godly sorrow produces repentance leading to salvation, not to be regretted; but the sorrow of the world produces death"* (2 Corinthians 7:10).

Labor to stir and awaken your soul from slumber and self-indulgence. Your sins are a big deal. You willingly sinned against a Holy, Righteous, and Just God. This is no small matter. The angels who sinned were cast out from Heaven, without any hope of mercy from God, nor any chance or opportunity for forgiveness, even if they were willing to repent. Oh, let the mercy and goodness of God humble you to your knees in bitter tears, and bless Him that you have a Redeemer. You have a Savior who paid a heavy price for your exceeding sinful soul, and on whose blood you can plead for mercy, and by a timely repentance you can secure a pardon for your wretched soul. The angels who have sinned, do not have a Savior; they are forever lost! Shall you then take the mercy and grace of God frivolously. Then trample the Son of God under your feet and count the blood of Christ a common thing. You insult the Holy Spirit, by saying and thinking, "My sins are not a big deal." Your sins are very grievous, because they are committed against a Holy God, who showed His extreme and irreconcilable wrath, anger and hatred against sin, by bruising His Innocent Son on the cross without mercy. Shall He let you go free? One who does not acknowledge the grievousness of your sins, against His Holiness. Oh, break your hardened heart and give glory to God, by letting His grace melt your heart and cause you to bow down heavily for your wretched sins. Beat your chest in sorrow and bitter tears for collaborating with satan and the flesh in committing treason against your King. Let not your face be lifted up to heaven, until you have sincerely sorrowed for your grievous sins. For your sins have once again inflicted fresh wounds on the blameless Son of God!

In mourning and sorrowing for our sins, we must guard our hearts against self-pity for any pain or consequences incurred as a result of our sins. That's not godly sorrow, that's regret, which doesn't take us anywhere. Godly sorrow is to focus on our horrid sins, in the light of God's holiness, mercy, and grace. Which is enough to break any sincere soul into tears and sorrow for offending such a Holy God with our sins! It is not about the shame, humiliation and pain that your sins have caused, but the offences you have committed against a Holy, Loving and Gracious Father!

iii. **Confess Your Sins:** *"If we confess our sins, He is faithful and just to forgive us our sins and cleanse us from all unrighteousness"* (1 John 1:9).

What makes sin so abominable, is not the action itself, but the motive behind the deed, which is nothing but contempt of God, and an attempt to break His right to rule over our lives.

And so it is, with true confession. A confession that is only focused on obtaining forgiveness, and removing guilt, and freeing us to commit the same rotten sins again, is a shallow, insincere confession. Yea, it adds to our sins, the grievous sin of mocking God, which deserves swift justice from God!

The aim of true confession is not just forgiveness, but removal of that which separates us from our Father. In confession we seek to reestablish our relationship with Him, with the sincere intention of grieving Him no more with our filthy sins. True confession of sin goes beyond just obtaining forgiveness; it seeks a new heart from God, a renewed grace from God, a Holy Spirit breathed and inspired zeal to love, obey and serve Christ!

We can discern the quality and savory of a confession by its tone, and the frame of heart of the suppliant, which is betrayed by the aroma of his heart. When someone wrongs us, and they simply say, "I'm sorry," and expect a full pardon with this lousy apology, we know he is not truly sorry. He simply regrets the inconvenience his wrong has caused in depraving him of whatever benefits he gets from us. His apology is false and insincere. He is likely to commit the same offense as soon as he is forgiven. This is true of ourselves, when we wrong others and plead for their forgiveness with such a cold, "I'm sorry."

A true and sincere apology sounds something like this, "I am sorry for hurting you by... and I'll try my level best not to do the same thing again."

The pain caused is acknowledged, the wrong is mentioned by name, and a solemn commitment to reform is made.

The same is true of a sincere confession of sins before God. The pain you caused God is acknowledged, each sin confessed by name, and by God's grace, a promise and solemn commitment to reform and forsake all sins is made.

Before you confess your sins and ask for forgiveness, think deeply of the grief you have caused God. Thoroughly search your heart for any unconfessed sins. When you are done searching the dark corners of your heart with your lantern—the eyes of your heart—Call upon God to search and scrutinize your heart with the sun of His piercing eyes, which reach the bottom of our hearts, even in areas we are too afraid to look. And as God reveals the hidden sins in your heart, give glory to God, by timely repenting of anything the Holy Spirit brings to light. Name your sins before God; grieve, weep, mourn over them before the throne of grace, and plead with God to uproot your sins from your heart. No one can approach the throne of grace with such a sincere confessing spirit, and return empty handed. God doesn't just forgive such souls, but He is well pleased also to renew their grace!

iv. **Plead with God to Cleanse You of All Your Sins:** *"The blood of Jesus Christ His Son cleanses us from all sin" (1 John 1:7).*

Sin always leaves a crimson stain on our cleansed souls, which defaces the image of God, stamped on our soul by the Holy Spirit at our conversion. The stains of sin make the image of Christ on our souls, blurred. Sin gives satan an opportunity to rebrand his image on our souls. Hence, to wallow in sins, is to allow the devil to rebrand you as his own slave; while living in sin, you think, talk, act, and live like the devil; making you the very image of the devil; so that, looking at you, is almost the same as looking at the devil.

In order to remove any marks and satan's likeness sin leaves in our souls, we need to be washed with a cleansing agent, powerful enough to remove the stubborn and resistant stain of sin. All our tears, regret, resolutions, and confessing are insufficient to blot away the tenacious spots sin leaves in our souls. Only the powerful, all-sufficient blood of Jesus Christ our Lord, can effectively cleanse the residue sin leaves on our souls.

Hence it is, that we find David, in Psalm fifty-one, after acknowledging the foul adultery he had commit with Barsheba; he publicly repents of it, humbly confesses it before God and the whole world, and then calls upon God to cleanse him of all the blemishes, stains, and residue his adultery left on his poor, righteous soul.

In his earnest plea to God to thoroughly cleanses his soul, David uses three distinct words or prayer *"Wash me,"* *"Cleanse me,"* and *"Purge me,"* – cried this child of God, under the severe anguish and guilt of his horrid sin. The adultery itself was a grievous sin. David, like some of us, aggravated his sin by attempting to cover it. He used his position of power, influence and advantage to hide his sin, adding hypocrisy to his already grievous sin and causing the stench of his sin to reach Heaven. David provoked the swift judgment of God to fall on him and his kingdom!

Therefore, God heard his pleas, and cleansed his soul, white as snow. However, because of hypocrisy, God did not blot this sin from the public record of his life. David's life is summarized thus:

"David did what was right in the eyes of the LORD, and had not turned aside from anything that He commanded him all the days of his life, except in the matter of Uriah the Hittite" (1 Kings 15:5).

Committing adultery and fornication, is a grievous sin in the eyes of God, it defiles the temple of the Holy Spirit; but murdering an innocent unborn child through abortion to cover your adultery or fornication, is a heinous, aggravating and provoking sin against the Most High! Should we be surprised when God's chastening rod hits us swiftly, after committing such evil?

Killing to cover a theft, lying to get away with a sin, or any other like attempt to cover and hide our sins, instead of repenting and coming clean, is not just odious in the eyes of men, but abominable in the eyes of God, to Whom nothing escapes!

It is no wonder, after seeing his monstrous sins, in the light of God's holiness, David cries with a lamenting voice, *"Wash me ... Cleanse me,"* and *"Purge me."* And we should be wise to do the same, after we acknowledge, repent, forsake, and confess our sins by name, we must plead with God to cleanse us and remove the stain of sin from our souls. Then, the image of God may be immaculate in our souls, and the glorious beauty and splendor majesty of Christ may radiate in us and through us to the praise and honor of His glory, Amen!

v.   **Plead with God to Restore the Joy of His Salvation in your Soul:** *"Restore to me the joy of Your salvation, and uphold me by Your generous Spirit,"* (Psalm 51:12). Having our hearts sprinkled with the precious blood of the Spotless Lamb of God, Christ Jesus our Lord, and our consciences thoroughly washed with the incomparable water of grace from the Everlasting God; let us press forward to the throne of grace and bow our knees to the God and Father of our Lord Jesus Christ. Let us reverently make our supplication as David did, praying, *"Restore to me the joy of Your salvation, and uphold me by Your generous Spirit"* (Psalm 51:12).

Oh, what a priceless gift from God, is a purified heart and cleansed conscience! Oh, give glory to God, and extol and praise Him for His incalculable grace. Amen!

However, we must not rest content with forgiveness only; a purified heart and a cleansed conscience without the joy of the LORD's salvation, makes a weak soul. And a weak soul is prone to detour, fall, and wallow in sin again.

The strength of the redeemed soul is the joy of the LORD! A soul filled with God's joy can resist temptations, which a joyless soul would easily yield and fall into. A joy-filled soul can endure the trials and afflictions that crush joyless souls.

We are forgiven by God, and washed in the blood of Christ, so that we may live a fruitful life to God; which is impossible without the joy of the LORD.

Hence, we find David, after acknowledging his sin, he repented, confessed and pleaded with God to wash him; yet as wonderful as forgiveness is, this holy man is not fully satisfied until the joy of God's salvation is fully restored in his soul! Why? He answers with the following verse, *"Then I will teach transgressors Your ways, and sinners shall be converted to You,"* (Psalm 51:13).

This righteous man did not just repent and ask forgiveness so that he may feel good and happy; he wanted restoration so that he may become useful to God again.

Toward the end of his plea for forgiveness, his confession is impregnated with a deep desire to please and serve God. Therefore, we find him mightily calling upon God to renew the strength of his soul, which is the Joy of God's salvation. Consequently, after pleading with God, David expressed his motive for needing his joy in God restored:

a) **To Please God:** David's terrible fall has taught him not to put any confidence or trust in himself, but to totally cast himself on the grace of God, alone. And if he will ever please God, it will be at God's cost, that is, he must rely on God's strength to keep him from commit such foul sins again. David doesn't have the strength to keep himself from falling into such terrible sins again; hence, he pleads with God, "*Uphold me by Your generous Spirit*" (Psalm 51:12).

b) **To Serve God:** David, like the rest of us, knows that without the joy of the LORD, every spiritual duty becomes a burdensome task. Prayer becomes a burden to the soul, Bible reading, alas, is heavy to the heart. Obeying God becomes wearisome. Without the joy of God, the soul is so weak, it is unable to perform even the slightest spiritual duty. A joyless soul would rather be busy with "the work of God," than to be busy with God. Such a soul would rather do anything else for God, except what God really expects of us—fellowship with Him.

The joy of God's salvation is nothing but the countenance of God shining upon us. Salvation gives us assurance that God is well pleased with us, which in turn gives us the confidence to approach Him and have fellowship with Him. This refreshes the soul, renews, and increases the soul's vigor with each trip made to the throne of grace.

Our sins cause God to frown, our obedience causes God to smile. That is why when we sin, we run away from God; but when we obey, we are confident to approach God.

When we pray, "*Lord please restore the joy of Your salvation in me,*" what we are really saying is, "Lord, please don't hide Your face away from my weary soul. Please don't cut me off from presence, which alone can refresh my weary soul and give me strength to love and serve You, making me well pleasing in Your sight."

Our souls' delight spring from the assurance that God is well pleased with us; evidenced by a vital relationship we have with Him and manifested in delightful usefulness for Him on this earth. You remove those two from any believing soul, and that soul will become barren and joyless. Nothing removes God's gracious presence from our souls, faster than sin. And once the presence of God is gone, we become useless and unfruitful. Oh, there is no joy like the gracious presence of God! And there is also, no severe affliction and agony greater than the awful absence of God, to the believing soul, especially if caused by sin and rebellion!

To live in sin and open rebellion against God, is to wallow in an open sewage filled with human dung, while eating our own vomit and licking our fingers. What filth! Who can honestly expect the holy God to be near and smile at us, while we are wallowing in such abominable filth?

Oh, God, I am too ashamed to look up, covered in such filthy garments of sin. LORD, I acknowledge the iniquity of my sin. My heart is sore. For I willingly crucified Your Holy Son Jesus afresh, and put Him to an open shame with my sins. I have rebelled against Your Holy Spirit and grieved Him by refusing His guidance.

LORD, my soul is sick, and my spirit is broken, for I, through my sins, have given the wicked one, and all Your enemies an opportunity to blaspheme Your Holy Name... God, be merciful to me, a sinner! Please forgive me in the name of Jesus Christ, wash me with the blood of Jesus Christ, and I shall be whiter than snow.

Restore in me the joy of Your salvation, and give me grace to trust Your love and believe Your Word. Uphold me by Your strength, that I may not sin again.

Please give me grace to love You with all my heart, mind, soul and strength, and use me for Your glory, oh, my God; strengthen me once more, oh my God, that I may delightfully serve You again.

Make me well pleasing in Your sight, and be glorified in my life from this day forward. I pray in Jesus' name. Amen!

Meditation Time:

Scripture Reading: Morning: Luke 15; Noon: Psalm 51; Evening: Hosea 14.

Memory Precept: *"Do not be like the horse or like the mule, which have no understanding, which must be harnessed with bit and bridle, else they will not come near you"* (Psalm 32:9).

Memory Promise: *"Take words with you, and return to the LORD. Say to Him, "Take away all iniquity; Receive us graciously, for we will offer the sacrifices of our lips"* (Hosea 14:2).

Commitment to Obey the Precept & Having Faith on the Promise: No more running away from God. No more delaying repentance. From this forward, if I sin against God, I will timely and unreservedly confess my sins before God, and ask Him to forgive me and wash me with the blood of Jesus Christ, and move forward with my God. *"If we confess our sins, He is faithful and just to forgive us our sins and cleanse us from all unrighteousness"* (1 John 1:9).

Heart-talk: Pour your heart to God, be sincere and honest; tell Him how you really feel, not what you think is acceptable, just pour your heart without being superficial. (Use a different note page, if you need more space):

II

Forgetting the Past

"Brethren, I do not count myself to have apprehended; but one thing I do, forgetting those things which are behind and reaching forward to those things which are ahead, I press toward the goal for the prize of the upward call of God in Christ Jesus."-Philippians 3:13-14

One immense hindrance that keeps so many good Christians from enjoying a fulfilling walk with the Lord is the nagging guilt of our past sins and shame. Surely, we ought to be ashamed of our past and present sins.

However, the guilt I speak of is the lingering guilt. The guilt that hangs around even after we repent and confess our sins to God, and ask for forgiveness. That guilt continues to sting our consciences and steals our joy in the Lord; we walk around feeling defeated and down cast. Some even go so far as giving up on God, because they fear to mock God by playing the hypocrite. Hence, they choose not to pray or read the Bible, or, if they do pray and read the Bible, they do it with a heavy heart, because they think they are unworthy of having fellowship with a Holy God.

The hypocrite does not care whether he mocks God with his pretense prayer or Bible reading; so long as he receives credit as a saint among God's people, he sees nothing wrong.

A saint however, would rather not pray and read his Bible, than do it in a way that mocks God; that is the very proof that they are indeed Saints of the Most High God, because they honor God in their hearts.

However, our dilemma is not entirely our sins and shame, but our faulty perception of God. It is our lack of understanding of the Person of God that causes us to go about our lives with heavy hearts, leaking the joy of the Lord, until, if nothing changes, we eventually remove ourselves from the presence of God, because we believe that's what we deserve.

Our defective view of God makes us see God as a righteous judge with a red pen, constantly pointing and remembering our sins. How can we enjoy the presence of God with such an erroneous, misrepresenting view of the Blessed God? Beloved, God is not at all like that. God is a Loving Father. He doesn't look at any of His children with disgust, nor does He view us as chronic sinners. When God looks upon us, He always looks at us with love, mercy and grace; yes, even at our worse, He still look at us as worthy heirs of His Glorious Kingdom, through Christ Jesus our Lord, Amen!

God does not remember any of our sins, which we repented, and have asked Him to forgive.

God's grace is like a vast sea, roaring with waves of love and tossing with winds of mercy to bring the Christian to his everlasting home. When a Christian makes a conscious decision to cast himself on God's grace, God casts our sins into the depths of the sea of forgetfulness, so that neither Christians, nor *"The accuser of the brethren,"* that old serpent, the devil, may find them.

"Once as prodigals we wandered,
In our folly, far from Thee;
But Thy grace, o'er sin abounding,
Rescued us from misery.
Thou Thy prodigals hast pardoned,
Loved us with a Father's love;
Welcomed us with joy o'erflowing,
E'en to dwell with Thee above," James G. Deck.

This is not knowledge to be stored in the mind, and move on with our defeated lives. We must embrace it, aggressively believe with our hearts, and forcefully take our rightful position as forgiven sinners and heirs of salvation; dearly loved and accepted by our Heavenly Father, through Christ Jesus our Lord, Amen.

Lord, please forgive my unbelief; for far too long, I've entertained and embraced guilt of things I've asked You to forgive. From today forward, I choose to believe all my confessed sins are forgiven. Please restore in me the joy of Your salvation, and give me grace to accept and daily enjoy Your love, mercy and grace in Christ, in Jesus name I pray, Amen!

Meditation Time:

Scripture Reading: *Morning:* Philippians 3; *Noon:* Isaiah 43; *Evening:* John 15.

Memory Precept: *"Do not remember the former things, nor consider the things of old. Behold, I will do a new thing, now it shall spring forth; Shall you not know it? I will even make a road in the wilderness and rivers in the desert."* (Isaiah 43:18-19).

Memory Promise: *"As the Father loved Me, I also have loved you; **abide in My love**. If you keep My commandments, you will abide in My love, just as I have kept My Father's commandments and abide in His love. These things I have spoken to you, that My joy may remain in you, and that your joy may be full."* (John 15:9-11).

Commitment to Obey the Precept & Having Faith on the Promise: God loves me. No more doubting God's love and forgiveness. From this day forward, I refuse to listen to the lies of the devil. All my repented and confessed sins are forgiven. I choose to abide in Christ's love, and daily live a joyful life, by the grace of God; trusting in nothing, but the love, mercy, and grace of God in Christ Jesus, Amen.

"Who shall separate us from the love of Christ? Shall tribulation, or distress, or persecution, or famine, or nakedness, or peril, or sword? As it is written: 'For Your sake we are killed all day long; We are accounted as sheep for the slaughter.' Yet in all these things we are more than conquerors through Him who loved us. For I am persuaded that neither death nor life, nor angels nor principalities nor powers, nor things present nor things to come, nor height nor depth, nor any other created thing, shall be able to separate us from the love of God which is in Christ Jesus our Lord" (Romans 8:35-39).

Heart-talk: Pour your heart to God; be sincere and honest; tell Him how you really feel, not what you think is acceptable, just pour your heart without being superficial. (Use a different note page, if you need more space):

III

Renewed Grace

---

*"When Jesus had raised Himself up and saw no one but the woman,
He said to her, 'Woman, where are those accusers of yours? Has no one
condemned you?' She said, 'No one, Lord.' And Jesus said to
her, 'Neither do I condemn you; go and sin no more.'"*
-John 8:10-11

Disobedience always causes a breakdown in our relationship with God.

The guilt and shame we feel after sinning, make us temporarily lose our spiritual sanity, and drives us to foolishly attempt the impossible—to run as far away as possible from God. We should make peace with this truth:

"'Am I a God near at hand,' says the Lord, 'And not a God afar off? Can anyone hide himself in secret places, So I shall not see him?' says the Lord; 'Do I not fill heaven and earth?' says the Lord" (Jeremiah 23:23-24).

There is no place in this vast earth where God is not, even when we are busy sinning, His righteous eyes are upon us!

The secret of living a victorious Christian life is

complete obedience to the will of God.

Disobedience hides His face from us; obedience on the other hand causes His lovely face to shine upon us. Hence the commandment, *"Go and sin no more."* That is, now that you are forgiven, and you have accepted God's forgiveness, don't grieve Him again by sinning willfully.

"Depth of mercy! can there be Mercy still reserved for me? Can my God His wrath forbear? Me, the chief of sinners, spare? I have long withstood His grace, long provoked Him to His face, would not hearken to His calls, grieved Him by a thousand falls. Whence to me this waste of love? Ask my Advocate above! See the cause in Jesus' face, now before the throne of grace. There for me the Saviour stands, shows His wounds and spreads His hands, God is love; I know; I feel; Jesus lives, and loves me still." -Charles Wesley

I believe one of the main reasons God forgives us so freely, and constantly shows us undeserved mercy, is to affect and enkindle our hearts to freely obey Him, not just out of duty, but out of love and gratitude for His indescribable grace.

God first forgives us, then He commands us to obey Him. Indeed, no one owes God obedience more than those who have been forgiven by Him. Therefore, in our text today, we see them put together: *"Neither do I condemn you"* and *"Go and sin no more."* God provides forgiveness and commands obedience. These are simple rules of life for every sinner.

Forgiveness restores our confidence in God, obedience makes us useful to God; and from these two, we quench our deepest thirst for personal fulfillment.

"Alas, and did my Saviour bleed?
And did my Sov'reign die?

Would He devote that sacred head
For such a worm as I?
Was it for crimes that I have done,
He groaned upon the tree?
Amazing pity! grace unknown!
And love beyond degree!
Well might the sun in darkness hide,
And shut his glories in,
When Christ, the mighty Maker, died
For man, the creature's sin.
But drops of grief can ne'er repay
The debt of love I owe;
Here, Lord, I give myself away—
Tis all that I can do!"-Isaac Watts

Yesterday you accepted His forgiveness; today, by His grace, choose to walk before Him in total obedience.

O God, You have shown me great mercy; now I pray, please give me an obedient heart, and pour Your divine love into my soul, that I may love You indeed, by keeping Your commandments; in Jesus name, Amen!

Meditation Time:

Scripture Reading: *Morning:* John 8; *Noon:* Ephesians 5; *Evening:* Hosea 6.

Memory Precept: *"See then that you walk circumspectly, not as fools but as wise, redeeming the time, because the days are evil.*

Therefore do not be unwise, but understand what the will of the Lord is" (Ephesians 5:15-17).

Memory Promise: *"After two days He will revive us; On the third day He will raise us up, that we may live in His sight. Let us know, let us pursue the knowledge of LORD. His going forth is established as the morning; He will come to us like the rain, like the latter and former rain to the earth"* (Hosea 6:2-3).

Commitment to Obey the Precept & Having Faith on the Promise:

God has been merciful to me. I must by all means avoid anything sinful; and by His grace, I must stay away from anyone and anything which leads me to sin against my God. And if I am left all alone with my God, so be it! But by the grace of God, no more sinning willfully against my God.

Heart-talk: Pour your heart to God, be sincere and honest; tell Him how you really feel, not what you think is acceptable, just pour your heart without being superficial. (Use a different note page, if you need more space):

_____

_____

_____

_____

_____

_____

_____

IV

Committed Love

"If you love Me, keep My commandments." -John 14:15

In order to avoid any misconception and misunderstanding of what it means to love God, Christ here states plainly, what loving God entails—obeying His commandments. That simply means that any attempt to love God, must spring from a fountain of sincere obedience. It doesn't matter how zealous, pious or religious a person may seem, they do not love God, until they have decided to sanctify the Lord God in their hearts.

Loving God begins when we make a conscious decision to align our lives according to His perfect will; and out of our own will, we choose to obey God in everything. So long as there are areas in our lives which we restrict God's access, and we insist ongoing our own way, we cannot claim that we truly love Christ.

> "All for Jesus, all for Jesus!
> All my being's ransomed powers:
> All my thoughts and words and doings,
> All my days and all my hours.

"Let my hands perform His bidding,
Let my feet run in His ways;
Let my eyes see Jesus only,
Let my lips speak forth His praise."-Mary D. James

That is the anthem of a heart ablaze with flaming love for Christ!

The only way we can sincerely love Jesus Christ our Lord, is through committed love. Love is an action verb and cannot be expressed merely by words; we must add actions.

We learn to love Christ with a committed love, when we begin to apply certain spiritual principles:

i.   **Total Submission to the Total Will of God:** It may come as a surprise when you discover your heart, mind, and will don't quite agree on what is good for you. Your mind may agree that God is worthy of love and He deserves preeminence in your life, but your heart may disagree; your will would rather love "Self," than love God supremely.
      Therefore, before a soul can truly love God, these three (heart, mind and will) must agree as one. Hence the word of God declares that we ought to love God with all our heart, mind, spirit and strength. Our whole being must be involved in loving God, otherwise, it's lip service.

ii.   **Devoted Time:** Choose a time, and make it sacred by dedicating it to God. Then jealously guard your devoted time. Allow no one, or anything to interfere or rob you of your divine appointment with God. Dedicate your devoted time to nothing, but communion with God in prayer, Bible study, meditation, and listening to God.
      The best way to express our love is, to give the most important thing we possess, to those whom we claim to love.

The most important thing we all possess is time (life); and we all prove our love by the way we spend it.

We spend most of our time with the people or the things that we love the most.

It doesn't matter how many times we tell a person "We love them," or how much of everything else we give; so long we don't give them our time, we do not truly love them; the same is true concerning our relationship with God.

The ones that love God the most, are the ones that spend the most time with God. And I'm not here talking of pastors, evangelists, elders, missionaries, or people called into full-time ministry; but about every child of the Most High in the offices, shops, fields, factories, kitchens, schools, taxis, or any other profession we may find ourselves in.

We can all express our love to God by acknowledging His Presence wherever we are, involve Him in whatever we are doing and invite Him in whatever situation we may find ourselves in— good or bad. Thus, there is no valid excuse in any one of us, why we should not express our love to God, except that we don't truly love Him.

You are worthy oh Lord, of my sincere love. I am ashamed of how little I really love You. Draw my soul unto You, oh Blessed Savior, pour Your divine love into my heart, that my love for You may be pure, warm and changeless; teach me oh Christ, to love You with all my heart, mind, soul, and strength, I pray in Jesus name, Amen!

Meditation Time:

Scripture Reading: *Morning:* John 14; *Noon:* Joshua 1; *Evening:* 1 Corinthians 2.

Memory Precept: *"This Book of the Law shall not depart from your mouth, but you shall meditate in it day and night, that you may observe to do according to all that is written in it. For then you will make your way prosperous, and then you will have good success"* (Joshua 1:8).

Memory Promise: *"Eye has not seen, nor ear heard, nor have entered into the heart of man, the things which God has prepared for those who love Him"* (1 Corinthians 2:9).

Commitment to Obey the Precept & Having Faith on the Promise: I must learn to love God; and love Him truly. No more compromising on my devoted time with God. From this day forward, by the grace of God, I choose to wholehearted obey God, and uncompromisingly do His will. I choose to remain in His presence.
"You will keep him in perfect peace, whose mind is stayed on You, because he trusts in You" (Isaiah 26:3).

Heart-talk: Pour your heart to God; be sincere and honest, tell Him how you really feel, not what you think is acceptable, just pour your heart without being superficial. (Use a different note page, if you need more space):

_____

_____

_____

_____

_____

_____

V

Fellowship with the Divine

"Jesus answered and said to him, "If anyone loves Me, he will keep My word; and My Father will love him, and We will come to him and make Our home with him." -John 14:23

After setting forth obedience as the chief token of our love for Him, Christ makes an invaluable promise to the obedient soul; those who choose to sanctify and obey the Lord God of heaven from the heart, will be rewarded with nothing less than fellowship with the Triune God! God will reward the obedient believer, not with things or blessings, but with His Shekinah— His awesome Majestic Glorious Presence! The ultimate gift God can give to the believing soul. While having God's Presence with us, we'll have no need of anything else for our happiness. Having made Christ our precious possession, we have all things in One— God.

God, in His infinite wisdom created our souls with an innate and insatiable need to dwell in His divine presence. There are no substitutes for His Presence. As the great Saint of old, St. Augustine, said, "Our souls are restless, until they find rest in God"

The sentiment is trumpeted by the psalmist in the opening verses of the forty-second psalm:

"As the deer pants for the water brooks, so pants my soul for You, O God. My soul thirsts for God, for the living God. When shall I come and appear before God?"

When a believing soul makes a heart-decision to shut the door on his rebellion, begins to exercise godliness in the daily affairs of his life, and sets God as the supreme ruler of his heart by rendering Christ total obedience from the heart; such acts of obedience compel God to gladly give Himself to such a humble soul. And all consists, "In one good act of renunciation of all those things which we recognized did not lead to God, so that we might accustom ourselves to a continual communion with Him, a communion devoid both of vagueness and of artifice.

"We need only to realize that God is close to us and to turn to Him at every moment, to ask for His help to learn His will in doubtful things, and to do gladly those which we clearly perceive He requires of us, offering them up to Him before we begin, and giving Him thanks when they have been finished for His honor." -Br. Lawrence

Here is the staggering thing in Christ's promise; it's not the obedient soul striving to climb to heaven, but the very Heaven invading the innermost chambers of the obedient soul. As always, the Triune God does not come empty handed, but brings with Himself living waters, wine of gladness and bread of life that He may dine and converse with the obedient soul! Blessed be YHWH, our God, forever and ever, Amen!

"For thus says the High and Lofty One Who inhabits eternity, whose name is Holy: 'I dwell in the high and holy place, with him who has a contrite and humble spirit, to revive the spirit of the humble, and to revive the heart of the contrite ones'" (Isaiah 57:15).

And again:

"Thus says the Lord: 'Heaven is My throne, and earth is My footstool. Where is the house that you will build Me? And where is the place of My rest? For all those things My hand has made, and all those things exist,' Says the Lord. But on this one will I look: On him who is poor and of a contrite spirit, and who trembles at My word" (Isaiah 66:1-2).

Let's therefore not be satisfied with a mediocre and shallow experience, when the Lord has promised so much more, if we choose, by His grace, to live in complete obedience to Him.

Forgive me O Lord, for holding back complete obedience to You, and pretending that I don't know what you've commanded me to do. Lord, I've been satisfied with very little; my fearful heart is afraid to lose people and things, if I choose to completely obey You.

Please deliver me from my unfounded fears, and give me grace to render unto You wholehearted obedience, in Jesus name, Amen!

Meditation Time:

Scripture Reading: Morning: John 16; Noon: Isaiah 55; Evening: Psalm 42.

Memory Precept: *"Seek the Lord while He may be found, call upon Him while He is near. Let the wicked forsake his way, And the unrighteous man his thoughts; Let him return to the Lord, And He will have mercy on him; And to our God, For He will abundantly pardon"* (Isaiah 55:6-7).

Memory Promise: *"If you abide in Me, and My words abide in you, you will ask what you desire, and it shall be done for you"* (John 15:77).

Commitment to Obey the Precept & Having Faith on the Promise: God wants to have real fellowship with me. No more half-hearted seeking of God. From now forward, by the grace of God, I choose to deliberately set aside enough time to build a strong and vital relationship with God. I must be determined to find Him; and not give up until I have found Him in personal experience. *"And you will seek Me and find Me, when you search for Me with all your heart."* (Jeremiah 29:13).

Heart-talk: Pour your heart to God, be sincere and honest, tell Him how you really feel, not what you think is acceptable; just pour your heart without being superficial. (Use a different note page, if you need more space):

_____

_____

_____

_____

_____

_____

_____

_____

_____

_____

_____

VI

Fear of Failing God

"The steps of a good man are ordered by the LORD, and He delights in his way."-Psalm 37:23

One of the biggest stumbling blocks that prevents so many good Christians from living a life wholly obedient to God is the fear of failing God before the world thus bringing reproach to God's holy name. Consequently, the fear of being called a hypocrite cause many believing souls to shy away from living an openly consecrated life before the world.

This I believe, is their attempt to protect themselves (and God's name), in case they fall into a great public sin, and the children of this lower world reproach and ridicule the holy name of the Son of God on their account. They tremble at the very thought of being the instrument by which the devil and his children may use to cast mud on God's face, and trample on the Son of the living God. Many sweet Christians are living their lives in the valley of indecision, severely torn apart by their desire to whole obey God, and the fear of failing Him. Sadly, many opt not to go all the way with God, and remain undecided their whole lives, not knowing that in so living, they deny God the glory they owe Him; until one day the grave claims them, and they are no more. What a sad end for a life with so much potential, if in obedience was placed in the hands of the Almighty God.

Some Christians are so overcome by this fear they judge themselves unworthy to be called Christians and think it is better to live a life in sin, than to be known as a Christian that publicly failed God. Sadly, many die in that state of mind. They die in their sins.

What a tragedy, for one who was on his way to heaven, to turn and head towards hell, not because God said so, but because he judged himself unworthy of God's mercy and grace.

This notion of failing God is unfounded with no scriptural support. Nowhere in the Scriptures of Truth are saints keeping themselves from falling by their own power or strength. Abraham, Isaac, Jacob, Moses, David, Elijah, Paul, Peter, James, John, and all great post-biblical saints are all kept by the power of God:

> *"Who [**all believers**] are kept by the power of God through faith for salvation ready to be revealed in the last time"* (1 Peter 1:5).

There are no grounds for any believer to fear that they will fail or shame God and play the hypocrite.

In fact, this fear is evidence that you are a true saint of the Most High God! For the hypocrite cares not about the honor of God; so long as he is well esteemed by man, and people speak highly of him as a saint, he is satisfied. But the saint abhors the dishonor of God, and that is what constitutes him a saint indeed.

It is God who called us from darkness, saved us from our sins and enemies, and promised that He will keep us by His Almighty power unto salvation.

"*Now to Him who is able to keep you from stumbling, and to present you faultless before the presence of His glory with exceeding joy, to God our Savior, who alone is wise, be glory and majesty, dominion and power, both now and forever. Amen*" (Jude 24-25).

And the promise:

"*Fear not, for I have redeemed you; I have called you by your name; You are Mine. When you pass through the waters, I will be with you; And through the rivers, they shall not overflow you. When you walk through the fire, you shall not be burned, nor shall the flame scorch you*" (Isaiah 43:1-2).

And again He promises:

"*Fear not, for I am with you; be not dismayed, for I am your God. I will strengthen you, Yes, I will help you, I will uphold you with My righteous right hand. Behold, all those who were incensed against you, shall be ashamed and disgraced; they shall be as nothing, and those who strive with you shall perish*" (Isaiah 41:10).

Our part is to cast ourselves whole on God, render whole obedience unto Him, and wholehearted trust that He will keep us to the very end, Amen!

LORD, I am ashamed of my lack of trust in Your mercy, grace and promise to keep me unto Your Heavenly Kingdom. I repent in dust, and cast all my self-confidence away from me. Please forgive me for believing that my sins, faults and failures are greater than Your grace; please be pleased to forgive Your servant of this grievous sin of unbelief, and wash me with the blood of Your Holy Son Jesus Christ, and I shall be whiter than snow. Give me grace O my God, to whole obey You; and strengthen me to live a holy life for Your glory, in Jesus name, Amen.

Meditation Time:

Scripture Reading: *Morning:* Psalm 37; *Noon:* Galatians 5; *Evening:* John 10.

Memory Precept: *"I say then: Walk in the Spirit, and you shall not fulfill the lust of the flesh. For the flesh lusts against the Spirit, and the Spirit against the flesh; and these are contrary to one another, so that you do not do the things that you wish"* (Galatians 5:16-17).

Memory Promise: *"My sheep hear My voice, and I know them, and they follow Me. And I give them eternal life, and they shall never perish; neither shall anyone snatch them out of My hand. My Father, who has given them to Me, is greater than all; and no one is able to snatch them out of My Father's hand. I and My Father are one"* (John 10:27-30).

Commitment to Obey the Precept & Having Faith on the Promise: Christ is my all sufficiency; in Him I stand or fall. No more trusting in myself. No more relaying in my own goodness, or good deeds and resolutions. From this day forward, I choose to trust on Christ's righteousness alone. I choose to depend on God alone, to supply me with His grace to live a holy life. With Christ keeping me, I cannot fall; without Him sustaining me, I cannot stand.
"For we are the circumcision, who worship God in the Spirit, rejoice in Christ Jesus, and have no confidence in the flesh" (Philippians 3:3).

Heart-talk: Pour your heart to God, be sincere and honest, tell Him how you really feel, not what you think is acceptable; just pour your heart without being superficial. (Use a different note page, if you need more space):

VII

Leaning on God

"Abide in Me, and I in you. As the branch cannot bear fruit of itself, unless it abides in the vine, neither can you, unless you abide in Me. I am the vine, you are the branches. He who abides in Me, and I in him, bears much fruit; for without Me you can do nothing." -John 15:4-5

It is no secret; anyone of us who dares to be honest with ourselves, will, upon a quick self-examination trace all our regression to the neglect of our personal and private devotion.

The coldness of our hearts, the indifference of our souls toward God and anything spiritual, can easily be attributed to the neglect of our closets—prayer and Bible reading. God calls this, "Forsaking God."

All our spiritual decays begin with a departure from Christ in our hearts. It is possible, as it often happens, to keep on with our daily routine of sets of devotions, without engaging our hearts to it. To keep our bodies in a devoted posture, but with our hearts on something or someone else. What makes our devotions lively and acceptable to God, is the warm affections stirred in our souls toward Him; a deep and ardent desire in our souls to fellowship with Him. You remove that, all our devotions become nothing more than a dead worship, a sacrifice of a dead corpse, which is utterly abhorred by God.

In the Old Testament Dispensation, the priests were commanded to burn the entrails of the animal being sacrificed, on the altar, to God. The entrails, the inside parts, were commanded to be peculiarly offered and whole burnt to God. For they symbolized the affection of the person that was offering the animal on his behalf. Therefore, in the New Testament Dispensation, we are exhorted to:

"I beseech you therefore, brethren, by the mercies of God, that you present your bodies a living sacrifice, holy, acceptable to God, which is your reasonable service" (Romans 12:1).

"Living sacrifice" is used because God is a living God. God will not be served by mere profession of lips, and a dead posture of the body, without the lively affections of the heart. Such dead devotion spring out of duty, not of love.

It is mocking God, to speak words in His presence, while our heart is hovering around on the things and people that have our heart; to read our Bibles just to ease our conscience that "we have spent time with God." To our shame, we are glad when we finish our chapter reading, and are free to rush to do what truly has our hearts. And we, that were so cold in the closet during our devotions, are suddenly warm and enthusiastic with the things of this world! God be merciful to us for offering the Majesty Divine, the King of Kings and Lord of Lords, such an uncomely, cold, and indifferent worship. Pity us oh my God, pity us and quicken us according to Your Word, in Christ Jesus our Lord, Amen.

Unless there is such a heart-cry from deep within our souls, we shall soon fall again. If we continue to mock and contempt God with dead unwilling devotions, we will force God to withdraw from us His all-sustaining and refreshing presence. His absence will give us over to the idols of our hearts, since we deprive the Great God our warm affections it is only fair for God to depart!

Without Him, we can do nothing, our joy and peace is gone. His absence makes us barren and inevitably we fall back into our sins. We may even commit grievous sins, which have lifetime consequences!

Oh, shake off the sloth of your soul, and warm your cold heart by fixing your mind on Him who suffered such a gruesome death for your heinous sins! Meditate on His undeserving grace over your exceeding sinful soul, and let the mercy He has over you brake and melt your icy, hard, and obstinate heart!

Look intently at all the idols that are stealing your love and affection away from Him, Who died for your wretched soul; are these things or people worth you losing Christ's presence? Oh, take the sword of the Spirit and begin to violently cast all your idols out of your heart, which is the temple of God, as Christ violently chased out all the money-changers, and all who sold things in the temple of God.

Empty your heart of affection toward idols, and labor to place all your affections on Christ Jesus our Lord.

Behold, He stands at the door, waiting for you to empty the sanctuary of your heart, so that He may enter, and there alone abide with you and have fellowship with your soul. Blessed be Christ Jesus our Lord! He never comes empty handed. He always brings the bread of life, and the wine of joy of the Holy Spirit to revive and refresh your soul, and empower you. Through Him you may live a holy and victorious life, and be fruitful in the ministry He has appointed you to accomplish.

His command to you today is, *"Abide in Me, and I in you... for without Me you can do nothing."* As if the Lord is saying, "Place all your heart and affections on Me; let your heart, mind, soul, and strength be fixed on Me; let all your dreams and hopes be in Me. I will be your life. I will fill your heart with pure joy, unbreakable peace, and an all-fulfilling existence!"

Beloved, all this and incomprehensibly more is available to you, if you choose to abide in Christ. A once and for all act of resignation is all that hinders your relationship with Christ. Cast yourself completely with an undivided heart into His loving arms. And there find all your joy, peace, and strength to live the life that you deeply desire! The choice is yours.

"Abide in Me, and I in you. As the branch cannot bear fruit of itself, unless it abides in the vine, neither can you, unless you abide in Me," Says the Master, in John fifteen, verse four. Will you obey? I pray you do!

O Christ, my precious Jesus. You, the Lover of my soul. You are my life. Please forgive me for being so cold and indifferent in prayer and reading Your precious Word. Have mercy upon me oh my LORD, for mocking You every time I prayed with a divided-heart, and gave You a cold service, and for allowing my mind to wonder to things, people, and even on myself. O LORD, You know it all, for nothing is hidden from Your eyes. I repent of such dead service and worship. Please forgive me LORD, in the name of Jesus, and wash me with His precious blood from such horrible sin of mocking You with my cold prayers and Bible reading. Father, I want to abide in You, and You in Me; Lord, please be pleased to give me grace to abide in You. Please give me grace to enjoy spending time with You in prayer; and please give me grace to delight in reading Your Word. You, O Lord Jesus, are all I want, please open the eyes of my heart, and empower me to seek You till I enter Your presence in personal experience, and there abide all the days of my life on this earth, and forever more through all eternity. In Jesus name, I pray, Amen.

Meditation Time:

Scripture Reading: Morning: Romans 12; Noon: 1 John 2; Evening: Psalm 50.

Memory Precept: *"Do not love the world or the things in the world. If anyone loves the world, the love of the Father is not in him. For all that is in the world—the lust of the flesh, the lust of the eyes, and the pride of life—is not of the Father but is of the world. And the world is passing away, and the lust of it; but he who does the will of God abides forever"* (1 John 2:15-17).

Memory Promise: *"Call upon Me in the day of trouble; I will deliver you, and you shall glorify Me"* (Psalm 50:15).

Commitment to Obey the Precept & Having Faith on the Promise: It is Christ plus nothing. He is my life, and for Him alone I must live. No more will I give my love, affections, and time to idols. From this day forward, I must, by the grace of God, empty my heart of all its idols. I choose to crown Christ Jesus as the supreme and unchallenged Ruler of my heart.

"Yet indeed I also count all things loss for the excellence of the knowledge of Christ Jesus my Lord, for whom I have suffered the loss of all things, and count them as rubbish, that I may gain Christ. And be found in Him, not having my own righteousness, which is from the law, but that which is through faith in Christ, the righteousness which is from God by faith; that I may know Him and the power of His resurrection, and the fellowship of His sufferings, being conformed to His death, if, by any means, I may attain to the resurrection from the dead." (Philippians 3:8-11).

Heart-talk: Pour your heart to God, be sincere and honest, tell Him how you really feel, not what you think is acceptable; just pour your heart without being superficial. (Use a different note page, if you need more space):

_____
_____
_____
_____
_____
_____
_____
_____
_____
_____
_____
_____
_____
_____
_____
_____
_____
_____
_____
_____

VIII

The Victory of Faith

"For whatever is born of God overcomes the world. And this is the victory that has overcome the world—our faith. Who is he who overcomes the world, but he who believes that Jesus is the Son of God?"
-1 John 5:4-5

Blessed be the God and Father of our Lord Jesus Christ, for His unfathomable plan of salvation! Blessed Atonement!

God, in His infinite wisdom, made an eternal covenant with His Son, Jesus Christ our Lord. The covenant is that all the divine requirements pertaining to our salvation, the Father would require from the hands of His Son. In fulfilling the covenant, the Son should undertake to fulfil, two things:

i.   **Render the Father** perfect obedience on behalf of all those who would believe on Him.

God created Adam, innocent, with a pure soul and a perfect heart that reflected the perfect Law of God. In his state of innocence, Adam was endowed with sufficient grace not only to repel any temptation the devil might tempt him with, but he also was able to obey the commandment God gave him, with great ease. So, Adam did not sin because the devil was powerful, or the temptation too strong; in his innocent domain, he could with great ease overcome the temptation if he wanted to. Adam sinned, not out of weakness, but because he chose to willingly rebel against God.

God created Adam endowed with the ability to overcome temptation and made a covenant of perfect obedience with him. God demanded and expected perfect obedience from men.

In the covenant of perfect obedience, there was no repentance. "Sorry, please forgive me," was not an option.

If you only sinned once and never again in your entire life, you will still owe God the obedience of the sin you have committed. Your future obedience is due to your future existence. Tomorrow's perfect obedience cannot pay for yesterday's sin; for tomorrow's obedience is due tomorrow!

Now think about the multitude of our sins in the light of the Old Covenant, and you will see how it puts the whole human race in total despair and helplessness!

Therefore, when God made the New Covenant, He didn't make it directly with us; because the debt of our sins is infinite, and we are morally and spiritually bankrupt to fulfill our end of the covenant. Even though we-who-believe are in the covenant, God made the covenant with His Son. His Son alone can fulfil the demands of the covenant on our end, and full pay the infinite debt of obedience we all owe God. We enter the covenant as beneficiaries, not as covenanters.

Now, as stated above, the Old Covenant puts the human race in a perpetual state of misery. We needed a New Covenant. But before the Old Covenant could be taken away, God's justice demands that all the terms and conditions of the Old Testament be fulfilled, before a New Covenant is effected. Since we clearly can never pay our debts, God made a covenant with His Son, and God expected His Son to fulfill all the terms and conditions of the Old Testament. Christ had to fulfill the two things that Adam and the rest of us would forever fail to fulfil—upon repentance, render perfect obedience to God, and pay for all our past sins!

Since Christ cannot fulfil our part of the covenant as God, He had to be born of a woman, and willingly make Himself a participant of our race. As one of us, He must render to God perfect obedience during His entire earthly life. He was not to miss one mark or one jot of the law. He had to fulfil all the commandments precisely and perfectly. Anything less than perfection would be rejected by the Majesty on High. Therefore, concerning His mission of rendering perfect obedience to the Father, our Lord Jesus states:

> *"Do not think that I came to destroy the law or the Prophets. I did not come to destroy but to fulfill. For assuredly, I say to you, till heaven and earth pass away, not one jot or one title will by no means pass from the law till all is fulfilled" (Matthew 5:17-18).*

ii.   **Offer Himself as a Sacrifice** to God for the Sins of Adam's Fallen Race.

Our Lord Jesus also had to pay the penalty of all the transgressions against the Law of God, committed since men rebelled against the Great God who created him in the Garden of Eden. Every sin that every person ever committed is accounted for. We may forget some of our sins, but God's record is infallible; there is not one single sin which escapes His eyes.

We are utterly helpless to pay for our sins. All our tears, regret, misery, pain, suffering, affliction, and tribulation cannot atone for one single sin. Yea, we may combine all the righteous men and women that ever lived since man was created upon the earth, but all their holiness, righteousness, tears, lamentation, and suffering, cannot atone for one single sin! Why? Because all sins are primarily against the Holiness of God, which is the crown of all His other attributes.

All crimes are aggravated by the nature and status of the person on whom the crime is committed. When a thief hijacks the car of a regular person, he commits a crime. But if the same thief tries to hijack the president's car, his crime is aggravated, and becomes treason, deserving a far greater punishment than the crime he commits in stealing a regular person's car.

Every single sin is committed against the Holy God of Heaven, the Infinite King of Kings and LORD of Lords. Because God is infinite, all sins committed against Him, accrue infinite punishment. And since we are finite, we are disqualified, not only morally and spiritually, but naturally also. Our nature being finite, can in no way pay for the infinite penalty of our sins. Only He who is infinite as God, can pay the penalty of sins committed against an infinite God. Who would accept his written-off Ferrari to be replaced by a Ford, or his stolen diamond ring to be repaid by a silver ring? Yet, these are but imperfect illustrations. The debt of one sin is infinite when committed against an infinite God.

Christ dispatched the first debt—*perfect obedience*—during the spotless and blameless thirty-three years of His earthly life. He then proceeds to secure the fulfilment of the infinite penalty of all our sins. Christ finds Himself in an incomparable dark night, in that terrible, dreadful, unforgettable garden, called Gethsemane! Where the wrath of God against sin is poured upon Him without a drop of mercy. So great was the load of the penalty of sin over Him, that in agony He pleaded, "O *My Father, if it is possible, let this cup pass from Me.*"

Oh, do not ever, ever, ever try to rob the Precious Son of God of the reward of His suffering, by thinking you can atone for your sins by regret, tears, promises, resolutions, and all other follies and attempts like fasting from certain foods and worship on certain days. All these things may be good in their proper place, but to think you make yourself more acceptable to God by keeping them, it is an abomination to God!

Oh, prostate yourself on the floor and reverently utter, "Christ alone. By faith alone! By grace alone. To the glory of God alone! It is Jesus plus nothing. In Him alone I stand, or forever I fall."

Oh, break forth in a song, and shout at the top of your voice with the hymnal writer:

"Jesus paid it all, all to Him I owe;

Sin had left a crimson stain,

He washed it white as snow.

"Lord, now indeed I find

Thy pow'r, and Thine alone,

Can change the leper's spots,

And melt the heart of stone.

"For nothing good have I

Whereby Thy grace to claim;

I'll wash my garments white

In the blood of Calv'ry's Lamb.

"And when, before the throne,

I stand in Him complete,

'Jesus died my soul to save,'

My lips shall still repeat."-Elvina M. Hall.

Oh, blessed be the Savior of our souls, Jesus Christ our Lord, Amen!

For in that excruciating, humiliating and shameful cross, He once and for all paid the infinite penalty of all our sins! Glory be to God our Merciful Father, Amen!

On the cross, Death claimed Him as his own; the Grave proudly shut Him securely as her own. Hell celebrated, and evil rejoiced. But God be thanks, that He who sits on the Eternal Throne is not only Just, but also a Covenant-Keeping God! Hallelujah, Amen!

For when the Son obediently died for our sins, and lain in the grave, oh the power from on high, the Blessed Holy Spirit raised Him from the grave, and not only Him, but also all of us who by faith die and are resurrected with Him. Amen!

Beloved, Christ Jesus our Lord has fulfilled all the divine requirements of the Old Covenant that stood against us, and took them out of the way; making way for the Father to establish a New Covenant with us. The evidence that His *perfect obedience* and *sacrifice for the penalty of our sins* is accepted by God, is the Holy Spirit sent down from heaven as a guarantee that we truly have eternal life in Christ Jesus our Lord, Amen!

When God announced the Old Covenant to the Israel of old, in Mount Sinai, He thundered it from heaven with a voice that shook the earth, with lighting, thunder, fire, smoke, and darkness. When He brings

His Son into the world to establish the New Covenant, He also speaks. After removing all the obstacles that stood in our way, the Father gladly announces the New Covenant, saying: *"This is My beloved Son, in whom I am well pleased. Hear Him!"* (Matthew 17:5).

"Cease all vain and unavailing self-effort to try to please Me in your own power. Believe that My Son rendered perfect obedience on your behalf, and paid the infinite penalty of all your sins, and I will accept you, and I will be your God and you shall be my sons and daughters."

That is the victory of faith in Christ Jesus our Lord, Amen. It triumphs over our infinite debts and rests on the finished works of Christ!

Bless the Son of God, oh my soul, and forget not what Christ Jesus your Lord has done for you, Amen!

These two unclimbable mountains—*perfect obedience* and *infinite penalty of sins committed*—stood as a separation wall between God and us. Having climbed them, the strong Son of God, by the mighty travail of His soul, alone, carved a narrow way between these two heaven-reaching mountains, for us to pass thru on our way to God. Christ paved the narrow way with His own blood! So when the righteous and sincere soul stumbles, he may fall on Christ's own blood! By a timely repentance, the believing soul may get up again, wash in the precious blood of the Lamb, and continue his journey until he enters the gates of the Celestial City! Praise the LORD, oh my soul, for His mercies and loving-kindness. The righteous always falls on the blood of Christ, Hallelujah! Amen!

After creating a way and paving it with His own precious blood, Christ invites everyone who is seeking salvation, to enter His narrow way, and commands us to stay on it until we enter the gates of heaven.

The believing soul rejoices at the proclamation of such gracious invitation and takes Christ at His word. The believing soul responds by breaking down in genuine repentance of sins, turns away from all his sins, washes himself in the blood of the Lamb, and enters the narrow road of salvation; thus, begins his personal journey to the Celestial City!

The sincere soul must be a resolved soul. Because the Master, the One who trod the way first, bid us that we must: *"Sit down first and count the cost,"* because, *"Narrow is the gate and difficult is the way which leads to life."*

Why is the Way Narrow and Difficult?

Firstly: The way is narrow because it is a singular lane, fit to be tread by one person only making it a lonely road. The Christian must walk in it alone, like his Master did, and if he would have any company on the way, he must call upon his Lord.

Secondly: As it is common consent, and as Garnell teaches, the way is difficult because there are three mighty enemies standing on the way of the Christian headed toward Heaven. The Christian must confront these three mighty foes, and by faith overcome them; or timidly wander off the path; or cowardly turn back. The three enemies are: the devil, the world and the flesh.

The Three Enemies the Christian Must Confront on His Way to Heaven

i. **The fist enemy is the devil:** This cursed serpent of old and his demons have a malicious hatred against God and the children of the Most High. Christ calls this cursed spirit, "The god of this world," and Paul calls satan, "The prince of the air," and the Holy Spirit presents the devil as a mighty, subtle, and crafty enemy against God's people throughout the ages. Satan and his demons have three great advantages over us, which makes them very dangerous adversaries:

a) **They Are Spirits:** Their very nature ranks above ours, though now fallen and defiled, they retain their spiritual nature.

b) **They Are Invisible:** Their spiritual nature makes them invisible to our naked eyes. Making them very dangerous. They are around us, yet we are unaware. And he who cannot be seen by his opponent, has superior advantage over his enemy.

c) **They Are Tireless:** Unlike us, who after fighting with each other for a while, however much we may hate each other, we'll get tired and stop fighting; not because the hatred has ceased, but because our bodies of flesh need to rest and regain strength before they can engage in the fight again. But it is not so with the devil and his demons; they don't have a body of flesh like ours. Their nature enables them to engage in their malicious war against us, without relenting—twenty-four hours a day, seven days a week, three-hundred and sixty-five days a year!

The Three War-Strategy the Devil Uses Against the Christian

The devil has a quiver with three arrows only. He attacks every Christian in a very predictable way—*he tempts, accuses and persecutes.*

i. **Satan's First War-Strategy is Temptation:** The first arrow satan shoots against the Christian, is to tempt and lure the Christian to sin against God. And his aim is to get the Christian to willingly sin against God.

ii. **Satan's Second War-Strategy is Accusation:** The second arrow satan shoots at the Christian, is to accuse the Christian of his past and present sins. And his aim in this is to bring discouragement in the Christian's soul, which very often leads the Christian to doubt God, and His mercy, grace, forgiveness and love.

iii. **Satan's Third War-Strategy is Persecution:** The third arrow satan shoots at the Christian, is to persecute the Christian in various way—in health, family, possession, reputation, etc. And his aim in this is to scare and frighten the Christian from the narrow way, the only way that leads to salvation. Indeed, the devil has overcome many professors through persecution. Many have indeed turned back, or detoured from the narrow way due to persecution, to save themselves, family, possession, reputation and the like. However, the devil has learned from experience that persecution doesn't work well in his favor; in fact, it works against him; for: "The blood of the martyrs is the seed of the Church," says Tertullian, an early Church father.

The more the devil persecutes the Church of God, the more the Church grows, and the more pure it becomes, and therefore stronger; that is true of the individual Christian as well. And that is the only reason God allows the devil to persecute His children. It helps God's children to grow, become refined and stronger, and consequently, more useful for Christ in His war against the devil in this evil world. Persecution is the devil's last resort. He doesn't use it much; his preferred weapons, are temptation and accusation!

O God, I have heard the trumpet! The enemies are mighty, fiery, and bloodthirst! And the shield of faith, alone, can repel their fiery darts. Lord please increase my faith, and strengthen my fainting heart, that I too may be Your faithful soldier in Your war against the wicked one, and through faith have victory over him for Your glory sake. In Jesus name, Amen.

Meditation Time:

Scripture Reading: *Morning:* 1 John 5; *Noon:* Ephesians 6; *Evening:* John 3.

Memory Precept: *"Put on the whole armor of God, that you may be able to stand against the wiles of the devil. For we do not wrestle against flesh and blood, but against principalities, against powers, against the rulers of the darkness of this age, against spiritual hosts of wickedness in the heavenly places"* (Ephesians 6:11-12).

Memory Promise: *"Above all, taking the shield of faith with which you will be able to quench all the fiery darts of the wicked one"* (Ephesians 6:16).

Commitment to Obey the Precept & Having Faith on the Promise: Christ has obeyed God on my behalf, paid for my sins with His own life, and He has given me a new nature. By the grace of God, no more yielding to satan's temptations. No more entertaining his accusations. No more being afraid of his persecutions. From now forward, by the grace of God, I choose to fix my eyes on Christ, and on what He has done for me. I refuse to focus on myself, sins, faults and failures. My eyes must be on Christ's perfect obedience, and perfect sacrifice on my behalf.

"*And as Moses lifted up the serpent in the wilderness, even so must the Son of Man be lifted up, that whoever believes in Him should not perish but have eternal life. For God so loved the world that He gave His only begotten Son, that whoever believes in Him should not perish but have everlasting life*" (John 3:14-16).

Heart-talk: Pour your heart to God, be sincere and honest, tell Him how you really feel, not what you think is acceptable; just pour your heart without being superficial. (Use a different note page, if you need more space):

_____

_____

_____

_____

_____

_____

_____

_____

_____

_____

_____

_____

_____

_____

_____

_____

_____

IX

How Faith Overcomes the Three Enemies

"Above all, taking the shield of faith with,which you will be able to quench all the fiery darts of the wicked one." -Ephesians 6:16

How Faith Overcomes the Fist enemy, the devil and his Three Wiles

How Faith in the Christian, Overcomes the devil

In the war against this wicked, foul and mighty foe, faith leads the Christian out of himself, and bids him not to trust one inch on his own strength and resolutions in his war against satan. Therefore, the Holy Spirit through the Apostle Paul, commands us, *"Be strong in the Lord and in the power of His might"* (Ephesians 6:10).

That is, "Poor Christian, your enemy is a vile and wicked spirit, he is mighty and swift, therefore, he is too strong for you. So, throw away your strength, and lay hold of the strength of Christ, Who alone is able to overcome this mighty devil."

Lively faith is like a watchful watchman in the soul of the Christian. When he sees the enemy approaching, he blows the trumpet to warn of approaching danger or sudden attack; so that the army may get ready and use all its power to fend off the enemy. So must every Christian, who means to overcome satan, by faith call upon Heaven, and lay hold of God's strength, and repel the enemy by God's Almighty Power.

Four Ways the Christian Successfully Overcomes the devil

i. **By the Blood of the Lamb:** In Revelation twelve, verse eleven, we have the secret, *"And they overcame him [the devil] by the blood of the Lamb and by the word of their testimony, and they did not love their lives to the death."*

The most efficient and surest way to defeat and overcome the devil, is to have absolute trust in the precious blood of Christ Jesus our Lord. Nothing shuts satan's mouth, and leaves the devil powerless, like the precious blood of the Lamb! The devil has no argument or weapon whatsoever against the precious blood of the Lamb. The Blood leaves the devil completely disarmed.

ii. **By Putting on the Whole Armor of God:** The second step is, to *"Put on the whole armor of God, that you may be able to stand against the wiles of the devil"* (Ephesians 6:11).

What is the whole armor of God? What does the Holy Spirit mean, when He says, we must put on the whole armor of God? In plain terms, the whole armor of God is the Lord Jesus Christ. In Romans thirteen, verse fourteen, we are commanded, *"But put on the Lord Jesus Christ, and make no provision for the flesh, to fulfill its lusts."* Unless a soul is truly and genuinely born again of the Spirit of God, that soul has not yet put on Christ, who is the whole, and I may reverently add, the only armor of God. Without which, a soul is naked and disarmed; consequently, powerless against satan. Only he who is born of God can overcome satan, *"We know that whoever is born of God does not sin; but he who has been born of God keeps himself, and the wicked one does not touch him"* (1John 5:18).

iii. **By Prayer**: At the disciples' request, Christ taught them to pray, and in them, us all: *"Our Father in heaven... do not leads into the temptation, but deliver us from the evil one..."* (Matthew 6:9,13). That is, lead us away from temptation. In teaching us to pray, our Lord intimates that we should address that Glorious Majesty on High, as our Father! O, what a privilege to call the Holy, Glorious and Everlasting God, Father! In teaching us to call God, Father, in prayer, the Lord eliminates any prayer that doesn't come from His children. God only hears the prayer from His children. For, *"We know that God does not hear sinners; but if anyone is a worshiper of God and does His will, He hears him"* (John 8:31). The only prayer God hears from a sinner, is the genuine prayer of repentance.

The evidence that we are true children of God is that we have received the Holy Spirit, *"Now if anyone does not have the Spirit of Christ, he is not His"* (Romans 8:9).

The evidence that we truly have the Holy Spirit is our pious longing to talk to God through prayer; our yearning to hear from Him by reading His word; our desire to give ourselves to meditation and singing unto God.

If a soul claims to be born again, yet is a complete stranger to the throne of grace, such a soul must reconsider whether it is truly born of God or not.

Sincere prayer overcomes satan, because it puts God on the side of the Christian against satan and all his hosts. Beyond any doubt, he who has the Almighty God on his side, must of necessity win the war!

iv. **By the Word of God**: To make sure of his victory over satan and sin, the Christian must add to his prayer, reading and studying the word of God, *"Your word I have hidden in my heart, that I might not sin against You.* (Psalm 119:11). And, *"Take... the sword of the Spirit, which is the word of God"* (Ephesians 6:17). The Christian must not only engage satan in battle by the power of God, but he must also use the weapon of God, namely, the sword of the Spirit; the word of God. He who neglects the word of God, daily, must of necessity, have a very weak faith; which calls very faintly to heaven in the day of trouble, and is hardly heard. A strong and living faith that is mighty in calling upon God to engage His Almighty strength in our war against satan and sin, is a faith born out of reading and hearing the word of God: *"So then faith comes by hearing, and hearing by the word of God"* (Romans 10:17). And, *"It is written...,"* said Christ to this foul enemy, called the devil, *"Man shall not live by bread alone, but by every word that proceeds from the mouth of God"* (Matthew 4:4).

We would be wise to do the same. The Christian must have the word of God hidden in his heart, and on the tip of this tongue, ready for offense and defense against satan. The devil was created by the word of God; out of nothing, God called Lucifer into existence, and at God's word He can rend him powerless. Therefore, let's give ourselves to diligent reading and meditation of the word of God, that we may be able to effectively and successfully repel this wicked spirit.

How Faith Overcomes Temptation

Before we can overcome temptation, we must first consider that temptation itself is not sin; giving in, yielding to, and acting upon temptation, that is sin. Daily we are assaulted by the devil and his demons, tempting us to sin. In order to successfully overcome temptation, we must first consider:

i. **Temptation is Common to All of Us:** Every single Christian is tempted to sin, daily. Even the Lord Jesus Himself was tempted by the devil. It is how we respond to temptation that determines whether we sin or not.

ii. **God Will Never Allow Any of His Children to be Tempted Beyond What They Are Able to Bear.** So whatever temptations you may be facing, you are able to overcome them by the grace of God, if you choose to.

iii. **Submission to God is the Most Essential Key to Overcome the devil and all his Temptations.** It will be difficult, if not impossible, for any of us to overcome temptation while we live in disobedience and rebellion against God. Obedience to God is the key to victory.

iv. **Resist the devil.** Every day the devil tries to plant into our minds notions to sin. We must, by the grace of God, firmly and resolutely refuse to entertain any suggestions to sin. If we stop it in our minds, it will most likely not reach our hearts and bodies.

v.   **Flee from Any Temptation or Appearance of Evil.** Nowhere in the Bible are we told to fight temptation; rather we are commanded to flee from it. Aware of our weaknesses, we must make a conscious and resolute decision to avoid by all means necessary the pitfalls we usually fall into. Every person, place, and activity that usually leads us to sin against God, must be courageously cut off and resolutely and seriously avoided.

How to Overcome Accusation

Because of our sinful nature and guilty mind, we are more easily persuaded that we are sinners than we are saints; more prone to agree with the devil than to believe God's word. Easily discouraged, it is vital and imperative to train our fallen minds and doubtful hearts to believe what God says in His word. *"For if our heart condemns us, God is greater than our heart, and knows all things"* (1 John 3:20). That is, we are not even to trust our own hearts or our feelings, but whole stand on what God says; it is that simple.

So when the devil comes in like a flood, accusing you of your past and present faults, you must answer, "Yes, it is true, I have done that, and much more; but God, to Whom alone I must give an account for my life, has promised me in His word, *'If we confess our sins, He is faithful and just to forgive us our sins and cleanse us from all unrighteousness'* (1 John 1:9). I have repented and confessed all my sins to God, God has forgiven me, and He has also forgotten all my sins. As for my present faults and imperfections, He says, *'There is therefore now no condemnation to them which are in Christ Jesus, who walk not after the flesh, but after the Spirit'* (Romans 8:1). By the grace of God, through the Blood of the Everlasting Covenant, and the heavy price my blessed Savior, Jesus Christ, paid for my soul, I am in Christ! There is no more condemnation for me! So, get behind me satan! You are wasting your time. I refuse to believe you, a vicious liar; I choose rather to believe God, to whom it is impossible to lie, Who alone is Truthful, Just and Faithful. If God says, there is no condemnation for me, because I am in Christ, I choose to believe my God!"

Now to further shut satan's mouth, and zip it, do this:

i. **Renew Your Repentance**: If there are any unconfessed and unrepented sins in your life, search your heart for them, and ask God to search your heart for any sin, and deal with all your sins by a timely repentance, and by grieving before God over the sins the devil is accusing you of.

ii. **Confess Before God All the Sins satan is accusing You of:** Unreservedly confess all your known sins without making an attempt to excuse or justify yourself.

iii. **Ask God to forgive you and wash you with the precious blood of Christ.**

iv.   Believe and trust in God's forgiveness and grace.

v.   Live joyfully and gratefully before God.

How to Overcome Persecution

Perhaps one of the greatest fears in the Christian's heart, is the fear of denying Christ in times of persecution. "What if I have to go to court or prison for my faith? Will I choose my freedom over Christ or will I be faithful?" Contemplates our fainting heart; "What if God calls me to be a martyr; am I ready to die for Christ?" or, "What if I am called to lose everything—family, wife, husband, children, parents, possessions, reputation, career and the like; will I be able to choose Christ over them, or will I choose them over Christ?" All this and other fears are real in the heart of the true Christian; to deny their existence is to, "Make the Cross, no cross at all."

How then is the Christian to overcome his fears, and be true to Christ, in the midst of persecution:

i.   **Firstly**, we must bear in mind that it is God who chooses the martyrs. Though all Christians have their fair share in the sufferings of Christ, and their personal crosses to bear, God chooses among His children, the strongest (Not in themselves, but in God), to bear the greatest suffering. So, no weak and fainting Christian will be allowed to be tempted and tried with prison or death.

ii.   **God Gives Special Grace to Those Who Are Called to be His Witness in Prison and Death.** A grace and courage they don't usually know they possess until they are called to prison or death for Christ's sake. You may think that you are not strong enough to go to prison or die for Christ; but if you are chosen by God,

God will give you grace to endure all, and be faithful to the end for His glory.

iii. **God Will Never Allow Any of His Children to be Persecuted Beyond What We Are Able to Bear.** We must always remember, God has the devil in a lynch, the devil is not allowed to do as he pleases; only what God allows him to do. Therefore, we must train our minds and prepare our hearts with this truth, that we may stand in the day of persecution.

How Faith Overcomes the Second Enemy, the World, And Its Three Lusts

As the Christian endeavors, by the grace of God, to walk faithfully in his daily walk on the narrow way, he is constantly disturbed and interrupted by the world. Daily, the world calls the Christian to wander off the narrow way and join the world. The world is forever promising to reward the Christian handsomely in two major ways—to fulfil his ambition and to give him the pleasures of this life.

The World Promises to Fulfil the Christian's Ambition

Many God-fearing, honest and good Christians have departed from the narrow way to pursue their ambition in the world. Whether in career, business, sport, music, film, studies, and like. They have a talent, and the world promised to compensate them generously for their talent and abilities, and they have accepted the deal. Some indeed depart from the Church altogether. While others choose to remain in the Church, in body, but their heart is stolen away by the world. *"For where your treasure is, there your heart will be also"* (Matthew 6:21).

And here is the subtlety and peril of it all; some of our ambitions are not sinful at all, they are useful to the world, and sometimes even to the

Church; but they cannot be achieved while we walk the narrow way, it requires us to step out of the narrow way, and there lies the intricacy. The Christian must eventually, by necessity, choose between Christ and his ambition.

The World Promises to Give the Christian Pleasure

There are many pleasures in this life that are not necessarily sinful, but are deadly to our spiritual life. Many wonderful Christians, have lost the fire and zeal for Christ and His Church, by simple watching TV, engaging on social media, and other forms of entertainment inordinately. They used to pray earnestly, read their Bible religiously, and zealously share their faith with family, friends, colleagues, neighbors, and others. But today, they are almost ashamed of Christ and His Gospel. When a Christian chooses to spend most of his free time with nonbelievers, he or she has lost the fire of God.

To avoid any misunderstanding, let's stop here and state: *"Command those who are rich in this present age not to be haughty, nor to trust in uncertain riches but in the living God, who gives us richly all things to enjoy"* (1 Timothy 6:17).

God is not against lawful pleasures. It is the lack of temperance that is our woeful dilemma. Any pleasure that requires you to detour from the narrow way, is deadly; it will ultimately bring spiritual death! The Christian must eventually, of necessity, choose between Christ and some of his lawful comforts and pleasures.

Four Ways the Christian Successfully Overcomes the World

i. **By Believing in Christ Jesus:** It is impossible for anyone to forsake, let alone overcome the world, without believing in

Christ. *"Who is he who overcomes the world, but he who believes that Jesus is the Son of God"* (1 John 5:5)? We were born into the world, and some of us have spent most of our adult life in the world, the world is so deeply entrenched in us, that only the power of the Cross can set us free from the love of the world.

ii. **By Forsaking the World with All Its Pleasures and Pomp**: It is impossible to enter the narrow gate without forsaking the world. To enter the narrow way, the Christian must first narrow all his interests to one—Christ. He must choose between Christ and the world; and once he has made his choice, he will easily walk on the narrow or broad way.

iii. **By Holy Ambition and Spiritual Interests**: Wherever our ambitions and interests are, that is where our heart will be; and wherever our heart is, that is where we truly are. A Christian with a holy ambition to become holy and perfect in the ways of God, doesn't need much persuasion to walk in the narrow way; his own ambition, desires, and interest points him to the narrow way. Therefore, he doesn't have much time to entangle himself with the affairs of this life.

It is true, sometimes his "Weary steps may falter," discouragement and doubt may harass him, and the cares and distresses of this life press him down, and he may even trip and fall at times; but having chosen Christ above everyone and everything else, his heart is fixed on Christ; get up he must, and moving forward is the only logical option of his fixed heart. He knows the Lover of his soul, and the One whom his soul loves cannot be found anywhere else, expect on the narrow way!

iv. **By Finding Joy and Pleasure in Christ Alone**: If Christ doesn't eventually become enough for the Christian, the Christian will ultimately turn back, or detour from the narrow way. The world says "Don't put all your eggs in one basket," or "Diversify your investments, don't put all your hope in one place." The Christian cannot afford to do that. All his non-existent eggs, must be in one place—Christ. He must sell all, and invest it all in the One he at last hopes to possess, not only in this life, but also in the ceaseless life to come. Therefore, all his interests and hopes of enjoyment must be singular—in Christ alone.

To walk in the narrow way, we must train our heart, mind, soul, and spirit to find joy in spiritual things. It is the only way we can successfully overcome the world with his three extremely dangerous daughters, the Lust of the Flesh, the Lust of the Eye, and the Pride of Life.

How to Overcome the Lust of the Flesh

The lust of the flesh are those things which appeal primarily to our carnal senses and gives pleasure to the body: sex, food, alcohol, dancing, etc. To a carnal heart, which has never tasted better things from above, the fleshly pleasures of this evil world are as appealing as the mud is to the swine.

There is nothing wrong or shameful with our human bodies. God created our bodies and God is not ashamed for creating them. Sex within the context of marriage is a wonderful and honorable thing; eating and drinking can be done to the glory of God, and we can even Dance before God like David. Lust of the flesh is the misuse and perversion of that which God created for His glory and our good. Therefore, fornication, adultery, debauchery, drunkenness, gluttony, and all host of those can never please God.

Faith overcomes the lust of the flesh. Faith lifts up the Christian's heart to things above, and Faith pleads with God to sanctify the heart to do all things to the glory of God. When we set our hearts to please God, we cease finding pleasure in pleasing ourselves, which pours ice-cold water on the fire of the lust of the flesh in our heart.

How to Overcome the Lust of the Eye

The lust of the eye, are those things which please our sight. Things in which the only pleasure we can derive from, is seeing them. Such as gold, diamond, jewelry, treasures, expensive paintings, and the like. A rich man finds pleasure in seeing his treasure; a woman finds pleasure in seeing her expensive jewelry; and the art collector finds pleasure in seeing his precious collection.

Apart from giving pleasure to the eye of those who possess and earn admiration for owning these visual objects, there is nothing more these trinkets can do. An expensive diamond necklace has no meaning to a blind woman and a Da Vinci classical painting is useless to a blind man.

Faith overcomes the lust of the eye, by sturdily convincing the Christian to remove his eyes from material and visible items, and place them on spiritual and invisible things. It is a mystery indeed to the carnal eye!

To have victory over the lust of the eye, the Christian must cast away all his pleasing visible objects from his sight, and fix his inner eye on the Treasure of Heaven—Christ Jesus. Whose value not only surpass all the earthly treasures combined, but is unmeasurable! The eye that has seen Jesus, becomes blind to the trifling toys of this life.

How to Overcome the Pride of Life

The pride of life, is the much-coveted desire to gain honor, reputation and prestige from men.

The desire to be somebody in this world, is deeply entrenched in our hearts. Everybody desires to be somebody, to rate and to rank and to be respected by men.

The pride of life has sent many decent and moral people to hell, because it keeps men from believing in Christ Jesus.

"How can you believe, who receive honor from one another, and do not seek the honor that comes from the only God?" (John 5:44).

Faith overcomes the pride of life by teaching the Christian to humble himself before God and men. Faith teaches the Christian to make himself nothing and last, the lowest and insignificant in the eyes of God and men. Such notion is indeed scorned by the sons of this evil world, but delightful to the Christian.

The believing soul accepts whatever value God places upon him. And is content with whatever value, or brand of reproach the world may fix upon him. For having received his true value from God, the Christian cares not how he ranks in this evil world, nor what men think of him. We have victory over the pride of life, when we give up our right to be respected by the world and completely cease demanding our true value from men!

How Faith Overcomes the Third Enemy, The Flesh and Its Lusts

When we speak about "the flesh," we tend to think of our bodies, but that is not the case. Our sins excepted, there is nothing inherently wrong with our bodies. When submitted to the Holy Spirit, our body can be a useful slave. We need our bodies to pray, read the Bible, fast, preach, teach, help the poor, widows, orphans and so forth.

When the Scriptures speak about "the flesh," it is referring to that fallen nature within us. The nature which is averse and contrary to God; the nature who is always conspiring against all that is righteous and is constantly asserting itself as the supreme ruler of our being. A nature, desperately wicked and bent on evil and mischief, which is always plotting in usurping the throne of our heart from its rightful owner—God. A nature whose unbending moto is, "I don't need God, I can manage my life myself." That is "the flesh;" it is who we really are, or have become in our fallen state.

Of the three enemies the Christian must wrestle with while walking in the narrow way to heaven, "the flesh" is by far the most dangerous of the three. The devil and the world are enemies, seeking access to our soul by luring, tempting and enticing us to open the door of our soul to them. And so long as we resist and refuse to open the door for them, they will always lose. But, unlike the devil and the world, the flesh is an enemy within! And worse of all, it has access to our secret intelligence. When we are busy plotting against overcoming certain sins, lust and vices, the flesh is also in attendance in all our secret meetings. Like a skillful spy, the flesh gathers all secret intelligence and betrays us into the hands of our enemies. And that is why many good and sincere Christian live defeated lives until the flesh is severely dealt with.

The devil's fate is sealed. He has been irreversibly condemned to everlasting damnation and to spend eternity in the midst of the unquenchable fires of hell where, *"Their worm does not die and the fire is not quenched"* (Mark 9:44).

The world's fate is also sealed, everything in it will be burned with fire and turned to ashes, *"But the day of the Lord will come as a thief in the night, in which the heavens will pass away with a great noise, and the elements will melt with fervent heat; both the earth and the works that are in it will be burned up"* (2 Peter 3:10).

The flesh has also been judged and sentenced to crucifixion. God has warned, flesh and blood will not enter the Kingdom of God, *"Now this I say, brethren, that flesh and blood cannot inherit the kingdom of God; nor does corruption inherit incorruption"* (1 Corinthians 15:50).

The time for the devil's punishment is fixed. The time for the destruction of the world is also fixed. But the time of the flesh's crucifixion is now! Yet the flesh refuses to get on the cross; it begs for more time, and it is constantly negotiating and renegotiating its way from the cross.

Any Christian who is sincere and knows the plagues of his own heart knows how devilish the flesh can be against God. And what a mess and pain the flesh can cause in our lives and the lives of others. Oh, how the flesh does us and others much harm, when it remains uncrucified in us!

Sadly, and to our great and perilous demise, we tolerate the flesh in us. We even make excuses for it. If the flesh is not timely crucified, it kills us and the ministry God has given us.

As Tozer teaches, "It is the veil of our fleshly fallen nature living on, unjudged within us, uncrucified and unrepudiated. It is the close-woven veil of the self-life which we have never truly acknowledged, of which we have been secretly ashamed, and which for these reasons we have never brought to the judgment of the cross. It is not too mysterious, this opaque veil, nor is it hard to identify. We have but to look in our own hearts and we shall see it there, sewn and patched and repaired it may be, but there nevertheless, an enemy to our lives and an effective block to our spiritual progress... I am bold to name the threads out of which this inner veil is woven. It is woven of the fine threads of the self-life, the hyphenated sins of the human spirit. They are not something we do, they are something we are, and therein lies both their subtlety and their power. The self-sins are these: self-righteousness, self-pity, self-confidence, self-sufficiency, self-admiration, self-love, and a host of others like them. They dwell too deep within us and are too much a part of our natures to come to our attention till the light of God is focused upon them. The grosser manifestations of these sins, egotism, exhibitionism, and self-promotion, are strangely tolerated in Christian leaders, even in circles of impeccable orthodoxy. ...Promoting self under the guise of promoting Christ is currently so common as to excite little notice. Self can live unrebuked at the very altar. It can watch the bleeding Victim die and not be in the least affected by what it sees. Self can fight for the faith of the Reformers and preach eloquently the creed of salvation by grace, and gain strength by its efforts. To tell all the truth, it seems actually to feed upon orthodoxy and is more at home in a Bible Conference than in a tavern."

How the Christian Successfully Overcomes the Flesh

There are two ways available to us, in which we can overcome the flesh with its lusts, which are, death on the cross, and learning to walk in the Spirit.

i. **By Death on the Cross:** There can be no true freedom, and power over sin in our Christian life, until the flesh is truly crucified. The flesh is an enemy within us that must be acknowledged as such; it must be repudiated and put to death by a deadly crucifixion.

Faith overcomes the flesh by lifting up the eyes of our soul and fixing them on Christ. While we gaze upon The Perfect One, the Spirit of God flips the switch in our poor, empty and bankrupted soul, and turns on the light of the perfect Son of God. Such revelation stirs and provokes the true Christian to endeavor to become like Christ. It springs in us an earnest desire to Christlikeness.

The revelation of our un-Christlikeness comes to us as a shock, which prompts us to cry out, "Oh God, make me like Christ," and God's reply is always, "Get on the cross."

Until we reach rock-bottom in our struggle against sin, and are sick and tired of the results our uncrucified flesh is producing in us, and against us, we will never get on the cross.

Let us not fool around, the crucifixion of our flesh is an excruciating experience; nor let us think about crucifying ourselves, by denying and depriving ourselves of certain things, or even by inflicting pain upon ourselves. Such self-crucifying will not suffice, because of self-pity and self-love. God must do the crucifixion; our part is to deny and repudiate the flesh, get on the cross, and stay on the cross until God finishes crucifying us. Our choice and cooperation will determine whether the job gets completely done, half done, or it remains undone.

Be very careful of self-crucifixion. Just as it is physically impossible for any person to crucify themselves because both hands must be crucified for the crucifixion to be complete, so it is physically impossible for any of us to execute it ourselves; someone else has to do it, for the crucifixion to be complete. So it is with our spiritual crucifixion, someone other than ourselves must do it. And only God knows how to truly crucify us. And all He asks of us is to choose to die to the self-life, unreservedly surrender ourselves to Him and get on the cross and say, "Do with me, O Lord, according to Your perfect will. Make the death of Christ real in my life, and let the resurrected life of Christ spring and flow through my soul." Such heart-cry is indeed a hard-saying to the Christian who is still at ease, but to the one who is truly sick and tired of the flesh, sin, self, it is an echo to the cry of their own hearts.

After all is said, there is nothing left to be done, but for the Christian to choose to die, get on the cross and ask God to make the death of Christ real in his personal life. Insist that God finishes the job.

"The cross is rough, and it is deadly, but it is effective. It does not keep its victim hanging there forever. There comes a moment when its work is finished and the suffering victim dies. After that is resurrection glory and power, and the pain is forgotten for joy that the veil is taken away and we have entered in actual spiritual experience the Presence of the living God." A. W. Tozer.

ii. **By Walking in the Spirit:** There is only one successful way to live the Christian life, and that is to, *"Walk in the Spirit, and you shall not fulfill the lust of the flesh"* (**Galatians 5:16**). Which simply means, that we refuse to lead ourselves in anything, but choose rather to seek the guidance and leading of the Holy Spirit in everything. It is to live our lives in total submission and obedience to the Holy Spirit.

We fulfil the lusts of the flesh when we choose and insist on being in control of our lives and lead ourselves.

We bear the Fruit of the Spirit when we choose to be led by the Spirit; when we refuse to think, say or act in everything without first asking the Holy Spirit for guidance and help. It is a life totally dependent on God.

It is a way of life which can only be learned by renouncing our will and diligently pursuing to do the will of God.

God knows who we are; God is not seeking perfection from us, while we live in this evil world. All that God is seeking from us, is a deep sincere desire to be led by the Holy Spirit and a holy intent to do His will always. God will make whatever allowances He wills, to make up for our imperfect ways. So long as our will is fixed on doing His will, God will supply all the guidance and grace needed for us to joyfully live a victorious, fruitful, and fulfilling Christian life, which is His perfect will for all His children, Amen!

O Lord, how true is Your word, "Without faith it is impossible to please God." For far too long I have been content with very little faith, and the result has been defeat upon defeat. Father, I want to live a victorious Christian life, but there are enemies within and without; be pleased O Lord, to increase my faith that I may trust You in everything and obey You in all Your ways which brings victory to those who trust and obey You in everything, I ask this in Jesus name, Amen.

Meditation Time:

Scripture Reading: Morning: Hebrews 11; Noon: Romans 8; Evening: Galatians 2.

Memory Precept: *"Therefore, brethren, we are debtors—not to the flesh, to live according to the flesh. For if you live according to the flesh you will die; but if by the Spirit you put to death the deeds of the body, you will live"* (Romans 8:12-13).

Memory Promise: *"A little while longer and the world will see Me no more, but you will see Me. Because I live, you will live also. At that day you will know that I am in My Father, and you in Me, and I in you"* (John 14:19-20).

Commitment to Obey the Precept & Having Faith on the Promise: I must die to self, and end this life of failure and weakness. This life of sin-confess, sin-confess must end. No more delaying getting on the cross. From this day forward, I must pray earnestly to God, that He makes the death of Christ real in my life. That Christ may live His resurrected life in me, and through me.

"I have been crucified with Christ; it is no longer I who live, but Christ lives in me; and the life which I now live in the flesh I live by faith in

the Son of God, who loved me and gave Himself for me" (Galatians 2:20).

Heart-talk: Pour your heart to God, be sincere and honest, tell Him how you really feel, not what you think is acceptable; just pour your heart without being superficial. (Use a different note page, if you need more space):

_____

_____

_____

_____

_____

_____

_____

_____

_____

_____

_____

_____

_____

_____

_____

_____

_____

_____

_____

X

The Tenacity of Hope

"Now hope does not disappoint, because the love of God has been poured out in our hearts by the Holy Spirit who was given to us."
-Romans 5:5

Hope is the second gear of the soul; an invigorating phenomenal staying power that endows the believing soul to climb the mountain of uncertainty, and walk in a higher terrain; the road of long waiting, with full assurance of obtaining the object of its hope. Hope is not faith; the two overlap and are inseparable from each other, but they are very distinct from each other. Faith produces hope, and hope keeps faith alive. They are interdependent of each other. Hope grows on the fertile ground of faith; and faith grows through the irrigation of the gentle rain of hope infused into the soul. There can be no hope without faith, and faith without hope will eventually die.

The Difference Between Faith and Hope

The difference between faith and hope lies on the object on which each rest. Faith rests on the promises of God. Hope rests on the character of the promiser—God. Faith believes the promise is true. Hope knows it will be fulfilled. Faith has its eyes fixed on the Word of God. Hope has its eyes fixed on God Himself. Faith is a gift of God that comes by hearing the Word of God. Hope is infused into our hearts by the Holy Spirit.

Types of Hope

There are two types of hope in the human heart: natural hope and spiritual hope. Their distinction lies solely on their extraction. One is earthily, while the other is heavenly.

i. **Natural Hope:** Is a rational hope based on the fixed elements of the universe, or the natural laws of the universe, as some call it. It is a hope that leans heavily on our own human understanding and rests greatly on the beggarly elements of the world. Natural hope is acutely sustained only by the knowledge and experiences of past generations, and kept alive by our desire to improve and make it better. So long as the natural laws of the universe run its natural course, natural hope will stand its ground. The farmer works his ground, plants his seed, hopes for rain or irrigates it, and hopes the ground will produce crops. He may think very little of what goes on underneath the ground, and what transpires for the seed to become a crop. Yet he is hopeful. A young couple gets married and hopes to have children one day, because it is the usual course of nature. We go to school and get an education, hoping that someday it will guarantee us a job. Scientists use the fixed points of universe in their new attempts, hoping to create or discover new things that can be beneficial or destructive to the human race. Almost every day, someone in this vast planet earth, is combining things together, mixing them in a trial and error process, hoping to produce a new thing—such as medical, alimental, and technology.

Yet, this natural hope, is an ephemeral hope, which can easily be snatched from us. When the heavens withhold rain, the farmer's fields die, and his hope dies with it. When the young married woman's womb is unable to conceive, or keep a child long enough, or the young husband is unable to produce seed, their dream to have a child dies, and their hope dies with it. Scientists are frustrated by the lack of their expected results, and some are given up as impossible; while other ideas die with the ones who dreamed of accomplishing it, and our hopes of such things die with their death.

So, natural hope, though useful in its proper place, is detrimental, when that's all we have. Experience bears this out. The famine caused by draught in a previously fruitful land, epidemics killing millions of people unable to be met by the so-called advanced science and technology, are but a few pointers to remind us of our demise when putting all our hope on the vague natural hope.

Yet, perhaps, nothing makes natural hope vainer than that dreadful and monstrous mountain called death; an inevitable and irresistible enemy, of which natural hope is no match. The desire to live forever, is deeply entrenched in the core of our beings, yet our hope is dashed to pieces, with each gaze we take upon death, by its visitation upon our loved ones, friends, colleagues and neighbors. A sobering reminder that our inevitable turn is coming. A dilemma that has baffled the most brilliant and most learned minds that have crossed the bridge of time thus far. The two most important questions in life still stares us in the face: "What happens when we die? Where will we spend eternity?" These are questions too deep for vain natural hope to answer!

ii. **Spiritual Hope:** Is a heaven-born assurance, deeply rooted and anchored on the Only Immutable Being in the universe—God. Spiritual hope is an unfailing hope. A hope as sure as God is God. A hope unaffected by the beggarly elements of the universe, and untouched by circumstances. A hope that defies impossibility, and fearlessly stares death in the eye. A hope that swallows up mortality, and courageously crosses the bridge of time into eternity. A hope anchored on God alone, on Who He is. Spiritual hope does not exist by the soul holding on to God, but by the Indefatigable Everlasting Arms of God keeping the soul. This hope is a gift from God. A gift God gives to every true believer who truly believes on His Son Jesus Christ as the only means of having eternal life. A hope that springs out faith created in our hearts by the Holy Spirit sent down from heaven. Which is, "Christ in us, the hope of glory!" A hope so certain, that it can boldly say:

"God is our refuge and strength,
A very present help in trouble.
Therefore we will not fear,
Even though the earth be removed,
And though the mountains be carried into the midst of the sea; though its
waters roar and be troubled, though the mountains shake with its
swelling. Selah" (Psalm 46:1-3).

The Anchor of Spiritual Hope

As stated before, hope is a gift of God that springs up out of faith. Faith must necessarily become hope. When faith gets tired of climbing the high and difficult mountain of waiting on God, Hope must take the burden out of Faith's shoulders and carry it until it reaches the top of a high plain, where the promised is fulfilled; otherwise the believing soul would faint in despair and sink in doubt.

Now, out of all known attributes of God, there are eight in which our hope must be anchored until we receive the promise. Which are:

i. **The Righteousness of God:** When we say God is righteous, we mean He is righteous in the last meaning of the word. We mean He is absolute righteous. Which simply means, He always does what is right. Uprightness is who He is, without any variation or shadow of changing. Therefore, we can count on God to always do what is right in anything and everything concerning us. We must train our hearts to rest on the righteousness of God, and always expect that God will do that which is right for His glory and our good.

ii. **The Truthfulness of God:** God is Truthful, Amen. He always speaks the truth. Truthfulness is His nature, it is impossible for God to lie. He puts His word above His name, because on His word, hinges the entire universe. All our present and future hope depends solely on the truthfulness of God. There is no other guarantee, of why we should believe on the promises of God, expect that, He who promises, is True. And He can never be anything else other than True. Truthful, is who He is, not something He does. The second person of the Godhead is called "The Truth." Therefore, we must train our souls to learn to take God at His word. For God never promises anything He has no intention of fulfilling. We can rest absolute assured, that whatever God has promised us, He will make it good on His word, Amen.

iii. **The Faithfulness of God:** God is Faithful, Amen. When we say God is faithful, we mean, He can never, ever deceive or fail on what He has promised. Faithfulness is not something He aims at, but it's His very nature. It is who God is. God's perfection requires that He be faithful; without absolute faithfulness, God would not be perfect, and that is impossible. God is always, has always and will always be perfect. Unfaithfulness taints the character of any man considered upright. Such is inconceivable in the Unchangeable Deity! God is faithful for Himself. We may be unfaithful to God, doubt, and even give up on Him. Yet, He will remain faithful to what He has promised, He cannot deny Himself. God is faithful not because we are good, or because we deserve it, but because He wills that no word that proceeds out of His blessed mouth should return void to Him. Amen. We must train our hearts to hope and rest on the faithfulness of God, by meditating that He will always accomplish what He has promised us, despite of us. He is Faithful for Himself first, and then for us. All his promises in Christ Jesus are yes and Amen!

iv.   **The Omniscience of God**: God is Omnisciently Perfect, Amen. When we say God is omniscient, we mean God knows absolutely everything there is to know; without any effort, God knows the past, present and future with absolute accuracy. There is absolutely nothing that surprises God. Yes, our sins, failures, rebellions and unwillingness are all well known to Him way before we were even born. So, when God makes us a promise, He makes the promise fully aware of our past, present, and future failures. Having perfect knowledge of our future stumbles and disobedience, God still makes the promise. The fulfilment of all His unconditional promises does not depend on us, or on our promises and resolutions to do good. After we have done our very best, it is still not good enough to qualify us to receive the fulfilment of the promise. No, God makes and fulfills His promises for Himself, and His eternal purpose for our lives, regardless of our failures. The fears that God will somehow change His mind, concerning something He has promised us, because we fail Him are unfounded. God never changes His mind. He makes His promises fully aware of all our failures. Our sins may surprise us, but not God. We must train our hearts to be hopeful in God, even at rock-bottom. We Trust that He who made the promise knew all about it before, and still freely choose to make us the promise; therefore, He will fulfil it, Amen.

v. **The Sovereignty of God:** When we say God is sovereign, we mean God is the absolute, supreme and unchallenged Ruler of the entire universe. No devil, demons, or evil men; nor angel, and nor good men can ever do anything without the ordained or permissive will of God. No leaf, flower, or hair of our heads falls to the ground without God allowing it. Whatever situation we may find ourselves in, good or bad, we can rest assured that God has allowed it. God may not initiate it, the devil and evil men may even intend for our hurt, but God only allows difficult situations to come our way for two reasons: His glory and our good. Now, since no one can do anything in the whole vast universe without God allowing it, we can rest assured, whatever situation we may be facing, God is in full control. We must train our hearts to see God in absolute control over our lives and circumstances. It is the definite antidote against murmuring, complaining, and rebellion against God, which never takes us anywhere, expect to stagnation in our relationship with God, and shame for playing the truant.

vi. **The Omnipotence of God:** God is Almighty, Amen. When we say God is Almighty, we mean, all power that there is, is His. It means His power is without limit and without diminution. God is as Almighty in this very moment, as He was before He created the heavens and the earth. He does not lose an ounce of power when He works; unlike man, who after some labor must rest to regain his strength. It means all power is His; and every power that exists, is derived from Him. All the power of the devil, demons, angels, evil, and good men combined is like a drop of the ocean in comparison to God's power. Therefore, God can never fail.

Sometimes good men with good intention fail us, because they are powerless to fulfill their well-intended promises. It is not so with God. There is absolutely nothing that can prevent God from fulfilling His promises. Without the least of efforts, God can quench and thwart all the power of the devil, demons, and evil men combined. God is always telling His people not to fear, since God has all the power to save, keep, protect, heal, provide, and more. We must train our hearts to focus on God's Almighty power when we are overwhelmed by circumstances. We must teach our heart to truly believe that there are no impossibilities with God. *"All things are possible with God."* There is no situation or condition that God cannot reverse. God can reverse even death when He wills.

O my soul, rest on the Almighty power of God, in Christ Jesus my Lord.
Amen.

vii.   **The Love of God:** God is love, Amen. When we say God is love, we mean love is who He is, His very nature. It's not something He does, or a feeling He has for a brief period of time, and changes when He is angry. God's love does not depend on our behavior, nor is it affected by our failures and sinfulness. From eternity, God willed to love us. Absolutely nothing, will ever change His will to love us. His love for us is as vast and infinite as God is. It never runs out, and it never gets tired. O, that our hearts would truly believe, *"Nothing can separate us from the love of God, which is in Christ Jesus our Lord."*

It is true, our sins and failure leave us ashamed to look at His lovely face. And our guilty conscience is forever ready to run away from God. Our unbelieving hearts is quick to believe our unworthiness, but very slow to believe that God truly loves us, personally.

It is true, we believe God loves everybody, but when it comes to apply God's love to us personally, we tend to disqualify ourselves. We must train our hearts to hope in nothing else, except in the love of God. When everything else fails, and we feel unworthy, we can always hope in His everlasting, unchangeable and infinite love for us in Christ Jesus our Lord, Amen.

viii.   **The Mercy of God:** God is Merciful, Amen. The foundation of our salvation is God's love; but the daily assurance of our acceptance before God, is His mercy. When we say God is merciful, we mean, that is who He is, His nature. It is not something He does, or some season in which He may be in the mood to show mercy. The mercy of God is as perfectly vast as God is perfectly vast. God's mercy is inexhaustible; it does not diminish because of our faults or the amount of our sins. His mercy towards us forever remains the same. One of the main causes of fear, doubt, and despair, which inevitably suffocates our hope, is our lacking of understanding of the mercy of God. We reason, because we have committed certain sins and failed God in certain areas of our lives, that God will also change and withhold His mercy and not fulfill the promise He has given us. Our reason leads to doubt and hopelessness. Only he who brings misery upon himself by his sins, is desperately in need of mercy, and is therefore the perfect candidate to receive mercy. The angels in heaven, and some "perfect people" on earth don't need mercy. The rest of us will not survive one single hour without the mercy of God. The need of mercy implies misery, and our sins always bring misery upon ourselves. We must train our hearts to hope on the mercy of God. In the midst of our sins, failures, imperfections, corruptions within and without, we must never doubt God's mercy. We must choose to look up to the God of mercy, and plead for mercy. We must never run away *from* God. We must always run *to* God, whatever our sins or circumstances, we must train our souls to cast ourselves on the mercy of God, and hope in His mercy alone.

How Hope Overcomes Fear

Most of our fears, if not all, spring up from our faulty understanding of the character of God. Though it is true, that it is impossible to know God in the last meaning of the word, yet in His mercy, God has revealed certain things about Himself that can be adequately known. We call these the attributes of God. They are reveled for our comfort and assurance. Most of our fears are unfounded. Hope overcomes fear by teaching our hearts to take our eyes from our problems and situations, and fix them upon the LORD God Almighty. The greater our hope in God, the less our fears will be. We must willingly and deliberately choose to fix our eyes on God and refuse to entertain the temptation of focusing on our problems. This never helps to bring about a solution; on the contrary, all it does is to magnify our problems, which increases our fear.

Our hope feeds upon God Himself, not on the promises. The greater our understanding of the character of God, the greater will our hope in God be. If that be remotely true, it would be wise of us to take time to study and get acquainted with God Himself. Such knowledge would dispel all our fears, as the sun dispels darkness upon its rising. One thing is certain, God wants us to serve Him without fear:

"To grant us that we, being delivered from the hand of our enemies, might serve Him without fear, in holiness and righteousness before Him all the days of our life" (Luke 1:74-75).

How Hope Conquers Doubt

Undealt with fear, inevitably produces doubt.

Doubt is to limit the Holy One of Israel. Doubt grievously dishonors God. Doubt never focuses on the promise, but on the Promiser—God. When we doubt, we make God a liar. Just as, *"Without faith it is impossible to please God,"* so we cannot doubt without dishonoring God.

As hinted before, the sole anchor of our hope, is the character of God. Doubt is a device of the devil, and it is always aimed at distorting our vision of the character of God. We never doubt until our view of the character of God is distorted first. Doubt has always an ill reflection upon God. Doubt greatly grieves God's heart, because no one can make us doubt. The devil may tempt us to doubt, but we don't actually doubt until we willingly give in and choose to doubt. That is why we are always greatly ashamed of our folly of willingly doubting God, when we come to our senses, and choose to repent, and trust God again.

Hope overcomes doubt by reminding the soul of the unchangeable character of God. Doubt chokes faith. Hope sets Faith free, and levels the ground. It is Faith's job to trust in the promises of God. Ultimately, doubt and trust are a choice of the will. No one can make us doubt. We can choose to trust God, or doubt Him. The choice is entirely ours.

How Hope Triumphs Over Adversities

There are seasons in our lives when our faith is constantly battered by trials, hardships, and temptations, and it is ready to quit. If hope does not timely come to the rescue of our faith, our faith will fail us, and adversities will prevail against us.

Some tests are pressing, straining and long lasting; some hardships are almost unbearable, some sicknesses and illnesses are lingering, and some temptations are extremely violent. And sometimes they all come upon our souls all at once. There are seasons when the Christian must face the chastening of God, the violent battering of satan's temptations, and the wantonness of his own flesh all at once. This sometimes prompts the soul to say like Jacob, *"All these things are against me"* (Genesis 42:36).

The tenacity of hope is revealed in the midst of our trials. When we are stretched almost beyond measure by circumstances, and pressed down by the failure of our own strength, hope saves the day by reminding the soul:

i. **It's Common to All Believers:** The sting of adversity comes from our inclination to give in to the temptation that we are the only ones that are going through such difficulties, and that everyone else seems to have it easy. God seems to answer everyone's prayers except ours. This inevitably brings discouragement. However, the Apostle tells us, *"Beloved, do not think it strange concerning the fiery trial which is to try you, as though some strange thing happened to you; but rejoice to the extent that you partake of Christ's sufferings, that when His glory is revealed, you may also be glad with exceeding joy"* (1 Peter 4:12-13).

Therefore, *"Be sober, be vigilant; because your adversary the devil walks about like a roaring lion, seeking whom he may devour. Resist him, steadfast in the faith, knowing that the same sufferings are experienced by your brotherhood in the world"* (1 Peter 5:8-9).

Hope triumphs in times of adversity by reminding us that trials are common to all God's people. All believers are facing the same, similar, or other types of chastening, trials, and temptations. Such news helps us to learn to be patient under our severest trials. When there is a famine in the land everyone bears it patiently. But if everyone else has food, and we are the only ones starving, it makes the sting of our hungry stomach almost unbearable, making our souls impatient. So, if everyone is going through it, and are learning to perfect their trust in God in the midst of their severest trials, some even far greater than ours, let us therefore learn to endure, and learn to patiently wait for God's deliverance, in Christ Jesus our Lord, Amen.

ii. **God Only Allows Adversities Which We Can Bear:** *"No temptation has overtaken you except such as is common to man; but God is faithful, who will not allow you to be tempted beyond what you are able"* (1 Corinthians 10:13).
God will never allow us to be tempted beyond what we are able to bear. All chastening, trials, temptations are regulated by the hands of our loving Father.
Hope again triumphs by reminding us that whatever circumstances, or situations we may find ourselves in, we, by the grace of God, are more than able to endure, and reemerge more than conquerors to the glory of God in Christ Jesus our Lord, Amen.

iii. **It's for a Limited Time:** No chastening, trial, or temptation lasts forever. There is a time when help from God arrives and we are delivered from our enemies and enter into a season of rejoicing, not only for the provision, restoration, healing or victory over sin, but also because of the awareness of the spiritual progress we have made, from the chastening, trial, and endurance of temptation.

iv.   **God Will Make It Work for our Good:** It does not really matter what our circumstances are; or how we got there. If we surrender and cooperate with God, God will make our circumstances (however bad) work for our good in the end. *"And we know that all things work together for good to those who love God, to those who are the called according to His purpose"* (Romans 8:28).

How Hope Surmounts Despair

Anyone who has been a Christian for a while, would sooner or later testify to their share of despair. A heart-renting season that tests our faith and patience beyond measure. Sometimes we face seemingly impossible situations, well over our heads, and way beyond our grasp. These may be an exhausting fight against a besetting sin that we cannot win, trying financial difficulties, a battle with a life threating illness, incurable disease, heath issues, heartbreaking family troubles, spiritual dryness and desertion, sudden loss of loved ones, loss of possessions, ministry difficulties and matters which we have no solution for, and find ourselves hopeless and downright despaired.

The Bible is filled with many examples of great men of God who fell into despair during their time of extreme testing. Elijah, the fiery and fearless prophet, in despair asked God to take away his life; Moses overburden with the task of ministry, asked God to kill him; David in the midst of his severe trials wished for wings so that he may run away from God. Our beloved Apostle Paul, tells us of his excruciating experience in Asia, which caused him and those with him to despair even of life, *"For we do not want you to be ignorant, brethren, of our trouble which came to us in Asia: that we were burdened beyond measure, above strength, so that we despaired even of life"* (2 Corinthians 1:8).

In the next verse, the Holy Spirit, through the Apostle Paul, reveals why Paul, Moses, Elijah, David, and many more of God's people despair, and sometimes even wish death upon themselves as a way of escaping the severe trials and seemingly impossible situations. "'Yes,' says Paul, *'We had the sentence of death in ourselves, that we should not trust in ourselves but in God who raises the dead, who delivered us from so great a death, and does deliver us; in whom we trust that He will still deliver us'*" (2 Corinthians 1:9-10).

We despair because we have such a high opinion of ourselves, making us confident in ourselves and abilities; and plainly put, we place a great deal of trust on ourselves. Since impossible situations, are really just that, "Impossible", our little ego of playing God of our lives is bruised, as we give in, and reluctantly accept our limitations. If we cannot solve the problem, who in the world can? The little god of our lives, called Self, would rather die with his pride intact, than to humble himself in trusting God with the impossible situation. Despair is trusting one's self in an impossible situation!

No one who surrenders an impossible situation to God should ever despair. That's why, little children, never despair. They fully hope in their parents. They may cry when they see us cry, and even for a moment be sad, because we, their hope, are in despair.

So it is with us, and our little god, "Self". When Self reaches its limit, we look at Self's face, and all we see is total helplessness. No wonder why we despair.

Hope triumphs over despair by teaching the heart to castaway all confidence and trust we have in self, and look up to God and place complete and absolute trust in God alone. The only remedy and cure for despair is having no confidence whatsoever in self. When that happens, despair vanishes. Total trust in God is the only solution.

Every time we feel the burden of an impossible situation weighing us down again, it is a sign that we are drifting from our trusting in God. We are trying to solve something we cannot solve. In the midst of our impossible situations, we must learn to say, "*Why are you cast down, O my soul? And why are you disquieted within me? Hope in God, for I shall yet praise Him For the help of His countenance*" (Psalm 42:5).

The habit will not be established overnight, but if we take the first steps, and persist in it, it will eventually become natural to us. We should not be discouraged if at first, we stumble and our trust in God is not perfect. If we persist in putting all our situations, and ourselves in God's hand, in due time our trust in God will be perfected. Amen.

O God, I am too ashamed to look up. For far too long I've been playing the God of my life. I repent in ashes, and castaway all my self-confidence and self-sufficiency. Please be pleased to forgive me of my lack of trust in You. Wash me from this grievous sin of unbelief with the blood of Your Dear Son Jesus Christ, and please give me grace to hope and trust in You more and more, in Jesus' name, Amen!

Meditation Time:

Scripture Reading: Morning: Romans 5; Noon: Psalm 146; Evening: Isaiah 64.

Memory Precept: "*Do not be like the horse or like the mule, which have no understanding, which must be harnessed with bit and bridle, else they will not come near you*" (Psalm 32:9). "*Do not put your trust in princes, nor in a son of man, in whom there is no help. His spirit departs, he returns to his earth; In that very day his plans perish*" (Psalm 146:3-4).

Memory Promise: *"For since the beginning of the world Men have not heard nor perceived by the ear, nor has the eye seen any God besides You, Who acts for the one who waits for Him"* (Isaiah 64:4).

Commitment to Obey the Precept & Having Faith on the Promise: *God acts for the one who waits for Him.* No more making plans for myself. No more relaying on my schemes for deliverance. And no more trusting in human beings. From this day forward, I choose, by grace of God, to put all my trust on God alone, and hope in Him only, and to wait patiently for God's deliverance.

"I waited patiently for the LORD; And He inclined to me, and heard my cry. He also brought me up out of a horrible pit, out of the miry clay, and set my feet upon a rock, and established my steps. He has put a new song in my mouth—Praise to our God; Many will see it and fear, and will trust in the LORD" (Psalm 40:1-3).

Heart-talk: Pour your heart to God, be sincere and honest, tell Him how you really feel, not what you think is acceptable; just pour your heart without being superficial. (Use a different note page, if you need more space):

_____

_____

_____

_____

_____

_____

XI

The Invincibility of Love

"Love never fails." -1 Corinthians 13:8

The great invincible force in the universe, is love.

Love is the epicenter of good; the spring of all things good. Love is the gentle shower rain that waters the hearts of men to produce good fruits out of an evil and corrupt nature.

When we think about love, we are usually inclined to think in terms of soft, tender, gentle, soothing, compassion, hearty, and the like. And it is good that we should think of love in such expressions; for love usually manifests in such ways.

Yet, as tender as love is, love is a force to be reckoned with. The enemies of love have learned through the centuries, to their dismay, that there is no strength like one motivated by love. Love has made men give up thrones of great kingdoms in order to be with the one they love. Women have abandoned a life of wealth and luxury to live in object poverty with the ones they love. Men and women have parted with their vital organs so that others may live. Love has even made people part with their own lives, so that their loved ones may live. Who can tell of what two people that genuinely love each other would do for one another? And what parents and children that love each other, would do for each other? There is no limit to what love would prompt a loving heart to do for the one it loves. Love is invincible because it never quits, never gives up, nor gives in.

"Love suffers long and is kind; love does not envy; Love does not parade itself, is not puffed up; does not behave rudely, does not seek its own, is not provoked, thinks no evil; does not rejoice in iniquity, but rejoices in the truth; bears all things, believes all things, hopes all things, endures all things. Love never fails" (1 Corinthians 13:4-8).

The sacrifice of Christ Jesus on the cross is the epitome of love demonstrated. The sacrifice of the Apostles and martyrs through the ages on crosses, stakes, sword, gallows, fires, and chains all for the love of God, is the echo of that love redounding back to the heart of Christ from which it first sprang.

What is Love?

Through the ages, poets, artists, high moral philosophers, theologians, monks, and mystics with their beautiful literature and art have in vain attempted to define and explain love.

What is love, then? Nobody knows. It is as impossible to define love, as it is impossible to define life. Love can only be demonstrated; it can never be defined or explained. All human attempt to describe and explicate love focus primarily on what love does, rather than what love is.

Love poems, love letters, love songs, and love stories are a relation of love in action, never love in definition. They all aim to help us understand what love is, by constantly resembling love to things more familiar and understood by our minds. Yet, after the poem, letter, song, and story ebbs away, we are right back where we have started, ignorant of what love is. They may strike a high note in our affections, and highly stimulate our emotions, yet never expound by definition what love really is in essence. It would be wise for us to stop here, as far as the definition of love is concerned.

The Bible does not define love for us, it says, *"God is love,"* but it never explains what love is. And one thing we are certain of, is that love is not God, but an attribute of God, like mercy, justice, and goodness. The only One who knows what love is in essence, is God. Yet, the Only Wise God, decided to demonstrate love to us, rather than explaining what love is, to our finite minds. We are unable to comprehend the simple things in life, let alone such a profound thing as love.

"For God so loved the world that He gave His only begotten Son, that whoever believes in Him should not perish but have everlasting life" (John 3:16).

When our Lord says this, He is demonstrating love in action; not what love is. I would simply say, love is the invisible and invincible force of good that keeps the rolling sphere in motion.

The Love of God

Let's bear in mind, when we speak of the love of God, we are talking of God's love in operation, not in essence. God's love is vastly perfect, and incompressible infinite.

The unshakable foundation of our relationship with God, is the inexhaustible love of God for us sinners, or rather, saints saved by the glorious love of the incomprehensible God! Amen. The love of God is independent of any external thing. All our Christian activities such as prayer, Bible reading, repentance, fasting, witnessing, and doing good deeds to our fellow men, enables us to experience God's love, but it never makes God loves us more. The love of God does not grow; it is already immeasurably perfect. Our love for God and others may grow, as we are transformed more and more into the image of Christ. God's love forever remains the same. God doesn't love us any more now, than He did before we repented of our sins, and by His grace amended our ways. It was His love that saved us, it is His unchangeable love that keeps us daily, not only when we have done everything right and fulfilled our duties, but regardless of what we have done, or didn't do.

The unavailing self-effort to earn the love of God by "Doing," has left many good people stranded in the valley of perplexity. God loves us, period. No need for any "ifs" or "buts" after that statement. Erase the thought that "God will love me if I become more holy, good and obey all his commandments," or "I think God loves me, but I am just not good enough; I'm always messing up." God loves you. That's where true Christianity begins.

I believe the only ones who truly experience God, and His love in personal experience, are those who truly believe that God loves them regardless, and approaches God in that way. Anyone attempting to fix himself, before he can approach God, will never experience the warmth of God's love. Imagine a loving mother withholding her love until her child has completed her chores! Imagine a mother who stops loving her child because she has misbehaved, or done something wrong? That's ridiculous!

Yet that's how we unfortunately view God; when we think He will love us more if we do this or that, or He has ceased loving us because we have committed a sin. We must wait until His anger is pacified before we can approach Him again. With such notions, is there any wonder why so few people experience God in marvelous ways, while others are left staggering in their unavailing self-attempts to please God?

Our Christian walk would become less perplexing, and our personal relationship with God less complicated, if we would just drop all intent to impress God and others; and recklessly dive into the ocean of God's love!

Different Types of Love

According to Saint Bernard of Clairvaux, a mystic who is believed to live around 1090 or 91-1153, there are four types of love. In his book "On Loving God," he explores the four types of love Christian's experience as they mature in God: *Loving one's self, selfish love, loving God as God, and loving one's self in God.*

i. **First Degree of Love: Carnal Love:** "Love is one of the four natural affections, which it is needless to name since everyone knows them. And because love is natural, it is only right to love the Author of nature first of all. Hence comes the first and great commandment, *'Thou shalt love the Lord thy God.'* But nature is so frail and weak that necessity compels her to love herself first; and this is carnal love, wherewith man loves himself first and selfishly, as it is written, *'That was not first which is spiritual but that which is natural; and afterward that which is spiritual'* (I Cor. 15.46). This is not as the precept ordains but as nature directs: *'No man ever yet hated his own flesh'* (Eph. 5.29). But if, as is likely, this same love should grow excessive and, refusing to be contained within the restraining banks of necessity, should overflow into the fields of voluptuousness, then a command checks the flood, as if by a dike: *'Thou shalt love thy neighbor as thyself.'* And this is right: for he who shares our nature should share our love, itself the fruit of nature. Wherefore if a man finds it a burden, I will not say only to relieve his brother's needs, but to minister to his brother's pleasures, let him mortify those same affections in himself, lest he become a transgressor. He may cherish himself as tenderly as he chooses, if only he remembers to show the same indulgence to his neighbor. This is the curb of temperance imposed on thee, O man, by the law of life and conscience, lest thou shouldest follow thine own lusts to destruction, or become enslaved by those passions which are the enemies of thy true welfare. Far better divide thine enjoyments with thy neighbor than with these enemies."

ii. **Second Degree of Love: Selfish Love:** "So then in the beginning man loves God, not for God's sake, but for his own. It is something for him to know how little he can do by himself and how much [he can accomplish] by God's help, and in that knowledge to order himself rightly towards God, his sure support."

iii. **Third Degree of Love: Pure Love:** "'*But when tribulations, recurring again and again, constrain him to turn to God for unfailing help, would not even a heart as hard as iron, as cold as marble, be softened by the goodness of such a Savior, so that he would love God not altogether selfishly, but because He is God? Let frequent troubles drive us to frequent supplications; and surely, tasting, we must see how gracious the Lord* is' (Ps. 34.8). Thereupon His goodness once realized draws us to love Him unselfishly, yet more than our own needs impel us to love Him selfishly: even as the Samaritans told the woman who announced that it was Christ who was at the well: '*Now we believe, not because of thy saying: for we have heard Him ourselves, and know that this is indeed the Christ, the savior of the world*' (John 4.42). We likewise bear the same witness to our own fleshly nature, saying, 'No longer do we love God because of our necessity, but because we have tasted and seen how gracious the

Lord is'. Our temporal wants have a speech of their own, proclaiming the benefits they have received from God's favor. Once this is recognized it will not be hard to fulfill the commandment touching love to our neighbors; for whosoever loves God aright loves all God's creatures. Such love is pure, and finds no burden in the precept bidding us purify our souls, in obeying the truth through the Spirit unto unfeigned love of the brethren (I Peter 1.22). Loving as he ought, he counts that command only just. Such love is thankworthy, since it is spontaneous; pure, since it is shown not in word nor tongue, but in deed and truth (I John 3.18); just, since it repays what it has received. Whoso loves in this fashion, loves even as he is loved, and seeks no more his own but the things which are Christ's, even as Jesus sought not His own welfare, but ours, or rather ourselves. Such was the psalmist's love when he sang: '*O give thanks unto the Lord, for He is gracious*' (Ps. 118.1). Whosoever praises God for His essential goodness, and not merely because of the benefits He has bestowed, does really love God for God's sake, and not selfishly. The psalmist was not speaking of such love when he said: '*So long as thou doest well unto thyself, men will speak good of thee*' (Ps. 49.18). The third degree of love, we have now seen, is to love God on His own account, solely because He is God."

iv.   **Forth Degree of Love: Perfect Love:** "How blessed is he who reaches the fourth degree of love, wherein one loves himself only in God! Thy righteousness standeth like the strong mountains, O God. Such love as this is God's hill, in the which it pleaseth Him to dwell. '*Who shall ascend into the hill of the Lord?*' '*O that I had wings like a dove; for then would I flee away and be at rest.*' '*At Salem is His tabernacle; and His dwelling in Sion.*' '*Woe is me, that I am constrained to dwell with Mesech!*' (Ps. 24.3; 55.6; 76.2; 120.5).

When shall this flesh and blood, this earthen vessel which is my soul's tabernacle, attain thereto? When shall my soul, rapt with divine love and altogether self-forgetting, yea, become like a broken vessel, yearn wholly for God, and, joined unto the Lord, be one spirit with Him? When shall she exclaim, 'My flesh and my heart faileth; but God is the strength of my heart and my portion for ever' (Ps. 73.26). I would count him blessed and holy to whom such rapture has been vouchsafed in this mortal life, for even an instant to lose thyself, as if thou wert emptied and lost and swallowed up in God, is no human love; it is celestial. But if sometimes a poor mortal feels that heavenly joy for a rapturous moment, then this wretched life envies his happiness, the malice of daily trifles disturbs him, this body of death weighs him down, the needs of the flesh are imperative, the weakness of corruption fails him, and above all brotherly love calls him back to duty. Alas! that voice summons him to re-enter his own round of existence; and he must ever cry out lamentably, 'O Lord, I am oppressed: undertake for me' (Isa. 38.14); and again, 'O wretched man that I am! who shall deliver me from the body of this death?' (Rom. 7.24). Seeing that the Scripture saith, God has made all for His own glory (Isa. 43.7), surely His creatures ought to conform themselves, as much as they can, to His will. In Him should all our affections center, so that in all things we should seek only to do His will, not to please ourselves. And real happiness will come, not in gratifying our desires or in gaining transient pleasures, but in accomplishing God's will for us: even as we pray every day: 'Thy will be done in earth as it is in heaven' (Matt. 6.10). O chaste and holy love! O sweet and gracious affection! O pure and cleansed purpose, thoroughly washed and purged from any admixture of selfishness, and sweetened by contact with the divine will! To reach this state is to become godlike. As a drop of water poured into wine loses itself, and takes the color and savor of wine; or as a bar of iron, heated red-hot, becomes like fire itself, forgetting its own nature; or as the air, radiant with sun-beams, seems not so much to be illuminated as to be light itself; so in the saints all human affections melt away by some unspeakable transmutation into the will of God. For how could God be all in all, if anything merely human remained in man? The substance will endure, but in another beauty, a higher power, a greater glory. When will that be? Who will see, who possess it? 'When shall I come to appear before the presence... Of the fourth degree of love: wherein man does not even love self, save for God's sake' (Ps. 42.2). 'My heart hath talked of Thee, Seek ye My face: Thy face, Lord, will I seek' (Ps. 27.8). Lord, thinkest Thou that I, even I shall see Thy holy temple? In this life, I think, we cannot fully and perfectly obey that precept, 'Thou shalt love the Lord thy God with all thy heart, and with all thy soul, and with all thy strength, and with all thy mind' (Luke n10.27). For here the heart must take thought for the body; and the soul must energize the flesh; and the strength must guard itself from impairment. And by God's favor, must seek to increase. It is therefore impossible to offer up all our being to God, to yearn altogether for His face, so long as we must accommodate our purposes and aspirations to these fragile, sickly bodies of ours. Wherefore the soul may hope to possess the fourth degree of love, or rather to be possessed by it, only when it has been clothed upon with that spiritual and immortal body, which will be perfect, peaceful, lovely, and in everything wholly subjected to the spirit. And to this degree no human effort can attain: it is in God's power to give it to whom He wills. Then the soul will easily reach that highest stage, because no lusts of the flesh will retard its eager entrance into the joy of its Lord, and no troubles will disturb its peace. May we not think that the holy martyrs enjoyed this grace, in some degree at least, before they laid down their victorious bodies? Surely that was immeasurable strength of love which enraptured their souls, enabling them to laugh at fleshly torments and to yield their lives gladly. But even though the frightful pain could not destroy their peace of mind, it must have impaired somewhat its perfection."

How to Love God

If we feel within our breast a deep longing for God, an acute desire to really love Him, and daily live in His presence, yet find ourselves frustrated and in despair at our inadequacy of truly loving God, we need not try harder to love and please God. A quick sincere look into the depth of our soul, in the light of the Scriptures will instantly deliver us from our dilemma. Just like in our human love, there are certain principles, qualities and commitments that help us to distinguish between those who truly love us, and those who don't; so, it is with our love toward God.

We love God:

i. **By Living a Pure Life:** Anyone desiring to have a genuine close and loving relationship with God, must decide very early in their pursuit, to endeavor, by the grace of God, to live a pure life. Without a great deal of purity of life, there can never be a manifestation of God's presence into our lives. And without the manifested presence of God into our lives, there can be no intimacy with God; and without intimacy, there can be no loving God on our part. Scripture says, *"Pursue peace with all people, and holiness, without which no one will see the Lord"* (Hebrews 12:14).

The first step in loving God, is to crisply set aside anything out of our lives that offends God, grieves the

134

Holy Spirit and has the potential to defile us. That is, anything the leaves us feeling guilty and indisposed toward God after we have indulged in it, must go; good or bad, it must go!

ii.   **By Obeying God:** *"If you love Me, keep My commandments"* (John 14:15).

The evidence that we truly love God, is the earnest desire, and actual willingness in our hearts to obey God in everything; coupled with grief, tears and godly sorrow when we fail to obey Him.

Any complaints against the commandments and precepts of God, is a sure sign of how little we love God. Though in this fallen state in which we find ourselves, we cannot render an absolute perfect obedience to God; yet, we can render a relatively perfect obedience to God. Even though, at times, we may falter in our endeavor to perfectly obey God in everything, God accepts our imperfect obedience springing up from the principle of holy intention to obey Him perfectly. Like a loving father who asks his child to fetch a heavy object, the father looks at the child with a bright smile and deep sympathy, rather than anger and displeasure.

iii.   **By Trusting God:** One of the main characteristics of true love, is the restless desire in our hearts to please the ones we love. It would be nearly impossible to convince the people we supposedly love, that we love them, without constant attempts on our part to please them. And so it is with our relationship with God. Any attempt on our part to please God, must begin with us learning to completely trust Him, as Scripture says, *"Without faith it is impossible to please God."*

We are not born trusting God. It is a conscious decision we all have to make at some point in our life. A deliberate decision, a setting of our will to expressly, voluntary and steadily place our trust in God, and on Him alone.

iv. **By Patiently Waiting on God:** The most difficult aspect in our Christian walk, is to wait on God. Nothing quite tests our faith and love for God, like long periods of waiting for God's deliverance.

Yet, waiting patiently on God, is the most holy, perfect, and pleasing act of worship we can ever render unto God! Having enough of waiting on God, is the number one reason why so many good and loving Christians never reach their destiny, and consequently miss the very best God intended to give them.

Let us not take this lightly, waiting on God is difficult, straining and exhausting. However, it is absolutely necessary for God to prepare us to receive His very best. Since God loses more people through blessings than through adversity, God as a loving Father, sometimes must withheld things from us until we are ready to receive and handle them; ready to use the blessing for God's glory, and ours' and others' benefit. And that can only be learned in the school of long waiting on God. *"[God] acts for the one who waits for Him"* (Isaiah 64:4).

v. **By Exalting God Above Everyone and Everything Else:** *"Be exalted, O God, above the heavens; Let Your glory be above all the earth"* (Psalm 57:5).

The ultimate test of love lies in the preference we give to the objects demanding our love. As it is often true, we feel loved when we are preferred above others, and we

Grace Restored

feel unloved when we are made second by the ones we expect love from. So it is with our love for God. The ultimate proof of our love for God will be evinced by the preference we give God when we have to choose between God over people, possessions, or ambitions. Our lack of love for God will also be revealed by the preference we bestow on people and things before God. As Dr. Tozer said, "Our break with the world will be the direct outcome of our changed relation to God. For the world of fallen men does not honor God. Millions call themselves by His Name, it is true, and pay some token respect to Him, but a simple test will show how little He is really honored among them. Let the average man be put to the proof on the question of who is above, and his true position will be exposed. Let him be forced into making a choice between God and money, between God and men, between God and personal ambition, God and self, God and human love, and God will take second place every time. Those other things will be exalted above. However the man may protest, the proof is in the choices he makes day after day throughout his life."

vi.   **BY reading and Meditating on God's Word Daily:** The adage, "The Bible is a love letter from God to mankind," should encourage us to cherish the Word of the living God. Love letters have been kept alive through the centuries, and have inflamed hearts with fervent love for objects near and far.

Our love for God germinates in our hearts by reading, hearing, and meditating on His word. It grows by the constant irrigation of living waters flowing through daily Bible studies and meditation. It is kept alive by meditating on the love of God widely spread across the Divine Pages. We read love letters because we love the ones who wrote it. There can be no love for God's word without love for God. When we truly love someone, we want to hear from them often. God expresses His love for us daily in His word. To hear God's loving voice speaking into the core of our hearts we must find a quiet place, open the Bible, read, and meditate on what God is saying to us in that particular moment. *"Oh, how I love Your law! It is my meditation all the day"* (Psalm 119:97).

vii.   **By Loving Others:** The proof that we truly love God, is our love for others. Our love for God is a raging sea, it cannot be hidden or contained; eventually, it spills over to others. Therefore the Holy Spirit through the apostle John says, *"If someone says, 'I love God,' and hates his brother, he is a liar; for he who does not love his brother whom he has seen, how can he love God whom he has not seen?"* (1 John 4:2).

viii.   **By Surrendering Our Will to God:** The goal of our redemption, is to make us like Christ. And to be like Christ is to willingly and delightfully relinquish our will to God. Which simply means to completely abandon and resign ourselves to the perfect will of God. It is the last thing God asks of us, and the most difficult to surrender. There are very few who live their Christian life in total abandonment to the will of God. Blessed are those who spend their whole lives in nothing else but in pleasing God! *"I delight to do Your will, O my God, And Your law is within my heart"* (Psalm 40:8).

ix. **By Rejoicing in God Himself:** *"Rejoice in the Lord always. Again I will say, rejoice!"* (Philippians 4:4).

Blessed is the soul who no longer finds joy in blessings and gifts, but in God Himself. Such a soul has attained, though not yet perfectly, the state of the blessed ones in heaven, who spend their blessed existence on gazing upon the Wonder we call God!

"Only to sit and think of God, oh what a joy it is! To think the thought, to breathe the Name; Earth has no higher bliss. Father of Jesus, love's reward! What rapture will it be, prostrate before Thy throne to lie, and gaze and gaze on Thee!" Wherever we turn in the church of God, there is Jesus. He is the beginning, middle and end of everything to us... There is nothing good, nothing holy, nothing beautiful, nothing joyous which He is not to His servants. No one need be poor, because, if he chooses, he can have Jesus for his own property and possession. No one need be downcast, for Jesus is the joy of heaven, and it is His joy to enter into sorrowful hearts. We can exaggerate about many things; but we can never exaggerate our obligation to Jesus, or the compassionate abundance of the love of Jesus to us. All our lives long we might talk of Jesus, and yet we should never come to an end of the sweet things that might be said of Him. Eternity will not be long enough to learn all He is, or to praise Him for all He has done, but then, that matters not; for we shall be always with Him, and we desire nothing more... I love Thee [Jesus] so, I know not how my transports to control; Thy love is like a burning fire Within my very soul.

"O Spirit, beautiful and dread! My heart is fit to break with love of all Thy tenderness for us poor sinners' sake." -Fredrick Faber.

"I want, dear Lord, a heart that's true and clean;
　A sunlit heart with not a cloud between.
A heart like Thine, a heart as white as snow;
　On me, dear Lord, a heart like this bestow."

"I want, dear Lord, a love that feels for all;
　A deep, strong love that answers ev'ry call.
A love like Thine, a love for high and low;
　On me, dear Lord, a love like this bestow."

"I want, dear Lord, a soul on fire for Thee;
　A soul baptized with heav'nly energy.
　A ready hand To do whate'er I know
To spread Thy light wherever I may go."

("A Heart Like Thine" by George Jackson)

Lord, I am too ashamed of my lack of love for You. It grieves my heart very deeply, that too often I have chosen people and things over You. I repent in ashes. Please forgive me for loving people and things more than You. Please wash me with the precious blood of the Lamb. Be pleased oh my God, to unite my heart to love You above everyone and everything else. Give me grace to exalt You in my life above all, in Jesus' name, Amen!

Meditation Time:

Scripture Reading: Morning: 1 Corinthians 13; Noon: Mark 12; *Evening*: Jeremiah 31.

Memory Precept: *"You shall love the LORD your God with all your heart, with all your soul, with all your mind, and with all your strength"* (Mark 12:30).

Memory Promise: *"The LORD has appeared of old to me, saying: "Yes, I have loved you with an everlasting love; Therefore, with lovingkindness I have drawn you"* (Jeremiah 31:3).
And:
"As the Father loved Me, I also have loved you; abide in My love. If you keep My commandments, you will abide in My love, just as I have kept My Father's commandments and abide in His love. These things I have spoken to you, that My joy may remain in you, and that your joy may be full"' (John 15:9-11).

Commitment to Obey the Precept & Having Faith on the Promise:

God loves me unconditionally. No more doubting His love for me. No more putting conditions on His love for me. From now forward, by the grace of God, I choose to love God above everything and everyone. I choose to exalt God above myself, others, and every created thing. I crown Christ the supreme object of my love. Jesus is the King of my heart, Amen.

"Who shall separate us from the love of Christ? Shall tribulation, or distress, or persecution, or famine, or nakedness, or peril, or sword?

As it is written: 'For Your sake we are killed all day long; We are accounted as sheep for the slaughter.'

Yet in all these things we are more than conquerors through Him who loved us. For I am persuaded that neither death nor life, nor angels nor principalities nor powers, nor things present nor things to come, nor height nor depth, nor any other created thing, shall be able to separate us from the love of God which is in Christ Jesus our Lord" (Romans 8:35-39).

Heart-talk: Pour your heart to God, be sincere and honest, tell Him how you really feel, not what you think is acceptable; just pour your heart without being superficial. (Use a different note page, if you need more space):

_____

_____

_____

_____

_____

_____

_____

_____

_____

_____

_____

_____

_____

_____

_____

_____

_____

_____

_____

_____

_____

_____

_____

_____

_____

XII

Walking in Christ's Footprints

"These are the ones who follow the Lamb wherever He goes. These were redeemed from among men, being firstfruits to God and to the Lamb" - Revelation 14:4

The sure way to get to our destination, is to follow close behind the One who knows the way—Christ.

Getting lost is inevitable when we insist on going our own way. There is only one way to enter heaven, and that is through the narrow gate.

God, in His divine wisdom, ordained that Christ should pave a way for us, out of this evil world, into everlasting glory. The Strong Son of God made a way for us, where there seemed to be no way. He climbed the high mountain of God's justice, crossed the sea of God's wrath, walked the valley of shame and humiliation, and unwaveringly treaded the straight line of God's perfect will, and entered the glorious presence of God on our behalf. Thereby leaving us His footprints for us to follow Him there. He paved the narrow way by walking it first. That He may uproot the pride of the human heart, the carnal fear of our souls and averseness of our hearts toward God. The way to heaven—the narrow way—is perfectly carved by the Son of God; it cannot be altered, nor can it be negotiated. He who intends to enter heaven, must not march through the wide and broad way. He must willingly break forth from the mould of the easy and broad way, and deliberately enter the narrow and difficult way carved and pioneered by the Champion of our faith, Jesus Christ our Lord.

We all, at certain point of our lives (sooner than later), must sit down with ourselves, and count the eternal cost of dying on the wide and broad way while carrying our Bible and making our prayers; while at the same time contemplating the hardships and difficulties that must be faced and endured on the narrow way, and make our choice accordingly.

One thing however that remains eternally true, is that there will be no one in heaven that reached and entered heaven through the wide, broad, and easy way.

Now to those of us who deeply desire to enter heaven and see God with our own eyes, we have no other choice but to count the cost, and decidedly enter the narrow way. We must follow in the footsteps of the beloved Son of God, and by the grace of God, we must stay on the narrow way until death transports us to the celestial city, or we are taken up to meet the Lord in the air, by the chariot of His mercy, at the second coming of Christ.

However hard and painful the narrow and difficult way may be, we must never turn back nor detour. Regardless of our failures, sins, and discouragements, we must resist the temptation of quitting the narrow way. Let those who love easy, have it easy. We must remain on the narrow way. It does not matter how many times we stumble or fall. If by the grace of God, we choose to remain on the narrow way, God will see us through, and it shall be well with our soul in the end.

The Blessedness of the Narrow Way

Blessed be the God and Father of our Lord Jesus Christ, Who in is His infinite wisdom, crafted with meticulous care the narrow way for the glory of His holy name, and the benefit and good of those who love Him enough to follow His beloved Son into the narrow gate, and walk all their lives on the narrow way for His glorious name's sake, and the blessed honor of our blessed Redeemer, Christ Jesus our Lord, Amen!

Why is the narrow way the only blessed way for the sincere soul to follow?

i. **It is the Perfect Will of God:** In plain terms, to walk on the narrow way is to give up all our God-given rights, freedom of choice, and lawful desires when they conflict the perfect will of God. It is a deliberate conscious decision that we make to stop leading ourselves, and in practicality let the Holy Spirit lead us in everything. No one can walk the narrow way by force. Because of our free will, we can only walk on the narrow way voluntary. Therefore, it is imperative that we completely surrender our will to God and allow the Holy Spirit to lead us in everything. We don't know the way or the obstacles and dangers on it. What seems good and useful today, can prove destructive and deadly tomorrow. The only successful way to walk on the narrow way, is to let God lead us in everything. Our hearts are forever coming up with schemes on what we can do for God. God doesn't want us to do anything *for* Him, God wants to do things *in* and *through* us. Anything we do for God will never be accepted in God's eyes. Our Lord says, *"I can of Myself do nothing. As I hear, I judge; and My judgment is righteous, because I do not seek My own will but the will of the Father who sent"* (John 5:30). To follow in the footsteps of Christ, and walk on the narrow way, is to "Not do anything of our own." We must cease and resist the urge and temptation to do anything out of our own resources. God must do everything; God must initiate, direct, and accomplish everything. Our part is simply to yield and be pliable in His blessed hands.

ii. **It is founded on the Love of God:** The very foundation of the narrow way, is the inexhaustible, unmeasurable, and unchangeable love of God. Any fear of us being forsaken while walking the narrow way is completely and absolutely unfounded. Holy Paul shouts at the top of his voice in announcing the inseparableness of the love of God and our souls, "Who shall separate us from the love Christ?" roars holy Paul, *"Shall tribulation, or distress, or persecution, or famine, or nakedness, or peril, or sword? ... Yet in all these things we are more than conquerors through Him who loved us. For I am persuaded that neither death nor life, nor angels nor principalities nor powers, nor things present nor things to come, nor height nor depth, nor any other created thing, shall be able to separate us from the love of God which is in Christ Jesus our Lord"* (Romans 8:35- 39).

iii. **It is Paved with the Precious Blood of the Lamb:** God knows the end from the beginning, and the intricacy of our fallen nature; He knows us better than we will ever know ourselves. God in His incompressible mercy paved the narrow way with the precious blood of the Son of His love, so that, if the righteous fall, the righteous must always fall on the precious blood of the unspotted Lamb of God. The righteous always falls on the Blood of Christ Jesus, hallelujah, Amen! Give glory to Him who alone is wise, for the precious, invincible and all-cleansing blood of Jesus Christ our Lord, Amen. God has taken all into account—the rebukes, chastening, and scourging to make us Christlike; the severe hardships, the sharpest pains, the fiery and violent temptations of satan, the intense luring of the world, and the unsanctified parts of our fallen nature, which every soul walking on the narrow way would soon or later face; God knew that such things would bring discouragement in our souls, which could lead to rebellion and sin. And ashamed the soul would have to return to God in repentance, desperately needing cleansing from such foul sins. *"Oh the depths of the wisdom of God! How unsearchable are His ways!"*

iv. **It is Hedged By the Truth of God on Both Sides:** Whether satan shoots his fiery arrows of temptation to cause us to sin, or the world enticingly calls the Christian to detour and enjoy the pleasures of this fallen world; or the flesh within begs for a little easy while the Christian walks on the narrow way; God has hedged the sincere Christian with truth within, and has set pillars of truth to hold the fences of the narrow way, to keep satan and the world out of the narrow way. Satan may roar from the sidelines, and the world may melodiously sing of its pleasures from the sidelines, yet they are both not allowed to cross the fence of the narrow way. The only way they can have access to the Christian, is when the Christian willingly steps out of the narrow way, by giving in to satan's temptations, or by listening and dancing to the world's tune. As for the flesh, the only way it can cause the soul to fall, is when we willingly listen to the flesh's suspicions of God's intentions toward us, and choose to believe the lies of the flesh, rather than the truth of God; other than that, the soul walking on the narrow way, is more than a conquer. So long as we stay within the hedge of God's truth, it shall be well with our souls.

v. **It is Roofed by the Grace of God:** The wrath of God is turned from all those walking on the narrow way. The justice of God cannot reach them because of the roof of grace erected by the merits of Christ Jesus. In the sunny days, they rejoice at His mercy; on the dark and gloomy nights, they rest on His unfailing faithfulness; on the despairing days of failure, they rest on His trustworthy promise of forgiveness; on rainy seasons, they take shelter under the indestructible merits of Christ. All our failures, shortcomings, detours, and sins are consequences of our pride, and can be traced at our unwillingness to call upon God for grace to help us through whatever strait, temptation, or luring that caused us to fall. As much as Self hates to be utterly helpless, and totally dependent on God, it will be wise for us to believe, and accept in the core of our being, that, *"Without Christ we can do nothing,"* without the grace of God, we are absolutely helpless, and totally disarmed against the slightest temptation of satan, the luring of the world and the corrupt inclinations of our flesh. *"Trust in the LORD with all your heart, and lean not on your own understanding; In all your ways acknowledge Him, And He shall direct your paths"* (Proverbs 3:5-6). Take shelter under the grace of God, always, put pride aside, and call upon God in the day of trouble, *"Call upon Me in the day of trouble; I will deliver you, and you shall glorify Me"* (Psalm 50:15).

vi. **It is a Living Way**: All other paths lead to dead ends; because they are dead paths. Through the ages, many paths, and religion sects have been created to bridge our return to God, yet all men's unavailing self-effort to reach and please God has been futile. God is a living God; the only way back to God is through a new and living way—the narrow way.

vii. **It is Filled with Angels of God:** The promise of God stipulated in Psalm 91:11-12, *"For He shall give His angels charge over you, to* *keep you in all your ways. In their hands they shall bear you up, lest you dash your foot against a stone,"* is literally fulfilled in our daily lives as we walk on the narrow way. Therefore, we are commanded to run the race set before us *"Looking unto Jesus"* (Hebrews 12:1-2). If our eyes are fixed on Christ as we walk, someone else must watch the way for us, and remove the obstacles and traps from our enemies. And that is exactly what the angels of the Lord do for all those walking on the narrow way. Countless car, plane, train, ship, bikes, pedestrian, and bicycle accidents are avoided by timely angelic intervention, at God's instruction. All those walking on the narrow way can testify of the myriad of times we have escaped and were delivered unharmed from situations which otherwise would leave us hurt and sometimes even dead. We cannot explain how we have escaped, but in the core of our being we know Who has delivered us, the Faithful God, Who has charged His angels to encamp around those who fear Him. *"The angel of the LORD encamps all around those who fear Him, and delivers them"* (Psalm 34:7).

The Three Callings of Christ

During His ministry on earth, the Lord Jesus has made three unmistakable calls to those who have ears to hear. The whole Christian walk is a personal response to these three life-altering callings.

i. **Fist Calling:** *"Come to me, all you who are weary and burdened, and I will give you rest"* (Matthew 11:28). That is, "Come out of all your unavailing self-efforts to please God in your own strength; and come rest in My finished work on the Cross for your sake, and I will give you rest."

"Take My yoke upon you and learn from Me, for I am gentle and lowly in heart, and you will find rest for your souls" (Matthew 11:29). That

is, "Put down your stubborn self-will, and pick up the will of God, and joyful carry it all your days. And you will find rest for your soul."

When the Bible speaks of the cross, the yoke, the narrow gate, and narrow way, It is simply using different terminology for our better understanding of the one and same thing, the will of God for our life. So, to reiterate it again, the cross, the yoke, and the narrow gate is the will of God for our lives. We pick up the cross when we refuse to do our own will and choose to do God's will. We take up the yoke of Christ when we refuse to initiate anything without God's instruction and help. We walk on the narrow way when we adjust our lives to be conformed to the perfect will of God.

In the first calling of Christ, we can distinguish two types of rest, the rest given, *"I will give you rest,"* and the rest found, *"You will find rest for your soul."* What is the difference? One is peace of mind, the other is peace of heart. We need both to have complete satisfaction in God.

Peace of Mind: Is the assurance we receive in our conscience that our sins are forgiven. Without such assurance, our minds are restless with guilt and fear. Peace of mind is a gift God gives to all who truly repent of their sins, place their trust on the atoning sacrifice of Christ on the cross for the forgiveness of their sins, and unreservedly confess all their sins to God and ask for forgiveness and beg for mercy. Yet there are millions of good Christians who have repented of their sins, and have received the assurance in their conscience that their sins are forgiven, yet find their hearts still restless. What is the problem? They have peace of mind but have no peace of heart.

Peace of Heart: Is the assurance we have in our hearts that God is well pleased with us. It is a gift God only gives to those who have taken up the yoke of Christ, *"I can of Myself do nothing"* (John 5:30). It is a peace that cannot be broke nor disturbed. It is whole unaffected by external circumstances. It is perfect peace. A peace only found in the hearts of those living the crucified life. Such great peace of heart is easily found by simply surrendering our will to God and learning to follow as the Spirit leads.

ii.   **Second Calling:** *"Follow Me"* (Matthew 4:19).   That is, "Turn away from leading your life and insisting things must go according to your own plans; resign from being the king of the castle of your heart and surrender the master plan that has been governing and guiding your life thus far, into the hands of God." Such surrendering, and blind following of Christ may seem reckless, and unreasonable to us at first. Perhaps, most of us wouldn't mind following Christ, so long as He would explain to us where we are going. However, as stinging as it is to Self, God doesn't owe us any explanation. All He asks of us is that we deny ourselves; step down from the throne of our hearts and crown Christ the supreme and unchallenged Ruler of our heart; pick up the cross and choose and accept the will of God for our lives and follow Him as He leads the way, one day at the time, one minute at the hour. We need not know where we are going, nor worry at what the future holds. As long as we follow close behind Him, we shall surely arrive at our blessed destination. "This way is called: In the Footprints of the Lamb. There we learn to understand the meaning of the Cross, to comprehend its power, and to walk in its shadow... The deepest meaning of the Cross is to give up one's own I." -George Steinberger.

In order for us to faithfully follow Christ, there are certain things that must take place in our hearts.

a) **An Earnest Desire to Please God:** Before we can begin our journey to follow Christ, there must be an acute desire in our hearts to please God. The purpose of Christ's mission to earth was to please His Father. He was made man, suffered pain, hunger, humiliation, ridiculed, and died on the cross to please His Father. That was His primary motive. And if we choose to follow Him, we must do likewise.

b) **Deny our Self:** It is easy to deny ourselves when an acute desire to please God is present in our heart. "He *'counted not the being on an equality with God a thing to be grasped,'* we read concerning Christ in Philippians 2:6. The deepest meaning of the cross is to deny one's own life. Paul expresses it thus: *'He died for all, that they that live should no longer live unto themselves'* (2 Cor. 5:15). We understand the meaning of the cross, and experience its power only when we can say with Paul, 'None of us liveth to himself' (Rom. 14:7).

"The fall of our first parents consisted in them making themselves the center of their life. The soul who does this today will learn that spiritual darkness and death, separation from, and enmity toward God, are the consequences of such choice. In all that is selfish, the power of satan is active there. In the selfish heart there burns the hidden fire of hell. As long as we cherish our own lives, we keep ourselves under God's curse; for on the cross God has cursed all that is selfish. 'To live for one's self' is to be against God. Our own "I" is synonymous with "flesh," and "the mind of the flesh is enmity against God" (Rom. 8:7). Flesh is ingrown selfishness. The selfish person desires to have all things for himself, desires to be the center of all things; and when this is not possible, he draws back, deeply hurt." George Steinberger.

c) **Live as Christ Lived:** *"For to this you were called, because Christ also suffered for us, leaving us an example, that you should follow His steps: 'Who committed no sin, nor was deceit found in His mouth'; who, when He was reviled, did not revile in return; when He suffered, He did not threaten, but committed Himself to Him who judges righteously"* (1 Peter 2:21-24). We can summarize the Lord Jesus' earthily life in this way, "He gave up all His rights that He may please and glorify God." And as George Steinberger concisely puts it, "On this Way the soul no longer complains: 'I am not understood! I am judged unfairly!' He, our High Priest, understands us, and this brings peace to our hearts. The sheep does not seek to be known and understood by others than its shepherd; it is enough for it to see his footprints, and hear his voice. When we follow the Lamb, there is nothing which can stand in our way or hinder our progress." Living as Christ lived, is to let the Holy Spirit live the life of Christ in and through us. It's not something you put on, and it cannot be faked. It is a glorious way of life that emanates from Christ in us. The manifestation of His resurrected life through our lives. "Today a minister wrote me: 'I can only be of blessing to my congregation when I live Christ before their eyes. I believe that this is the most effective kind of preaching. It has always attracted me personally and it still continues to do so. He who thirsts, gladly refreshes himself at a cool flowing fountain. And are not we called to be 'fountains'?" Yes, wells of living water! (John 4:14)." George Steinberger.

d) **Walk as He Walked**: *"He who says he abides in Him ought himself also to walk just as He walked."* (1 John 2:6). The unparalleled walk of Christ on earth, as recorded in the Scriptures, is designed to show us how to walk before God. Many things are recorded of Christ, but one thing that stands out, and towers above the rest, and comes out as the center focus of His life, is that He walked all His life on earth with His eyes fixed on the will of His Father. And if we desire to follow Him, it would be wise for us to do the same. Let us therefore walk the walk of life with our eyes fixed on the will of God, with an earnest desire to learn to do His will more perfectly with each day that passes.

iii. **Third Call:** *"Abide in Me"* (John 15:4). God created us to live in His presence. That is why there is a deep yearning for the presence of God in our hearts, who have been born again of the Spirit of God. Our souls will forever remain restless until we enter into the presence of God in conscious experience. As the sea is to the fish, so is God to our souls. He is our proper domain of abode. The promise, *"My Presence will go with you, and I will give you rest"* (Exodus 33:14); is a promise given to every child of the Most High. Why are some many of God's children living restless lives? They have not yet made Christ their abiding place. Abiding in Christ, is the ultimate solution for all our spiritual difficulties. What abiding in Christ can do for us, nothing else can. Abiding enables us to draw from the all satisfying life of Christ. Like the branch draws its life-giving sap from the tree, so our soul taps into the life of Christ when we abide in Him. And if we can have the life of Christ flowing through our soul, what else do we need? There are key benefits abiding in Christ brings about, which when carefully considered, should encourage us all the more to make Christ our abiding place.

a) **Abiding in Christ Brings Entire Satisfaction of our Total Nature:** The human heart is deep! There is absolutely nothing that can satisfy our deep hearts, but God. This we all know, and believe in theory, but somehow we find ourselves pursuing satisfaction on the very things we believe can never satisfy us. God, without anything else, is absolutely able to satisfy the deepest desire of our deep hearts. When we abide in Christ, God gives us Himself, by filling us with Himself, in such a way that we will have to beg Him to stop, lest our soul burst with the fullness of God!

b) **Abiding in Christ Brings an Unrivaled Satisfying Usefulness in the Kingdom of God:** The truism of the promise in John fifteen, verse five, *"He who abides in Me, and I in him, bears much fruit;"* is validated by the lives of many believers who have learned the secret of abiding. The unmatched amount of fruit they bear in their lives, is all the proof that we all need. There is no limit to the great things God can accomplish through a life deeply abiding in Christ.

c) **Abiding in Christ Brings Ravishing Knowledge of God:** *"This is eternal life, that they may know You, the only true God,* *and Jesus Christ whom You have sent"* (John 17:3). According to our Lord, eternal life is the soul's personal and experiential knowledge of God. The Church is saturated with doctrine, creeds, rules and regulations; do's and don'ts, stiff denominational standings, rigid enforcement of things unnecessary to salvation, and a sharp criticism of others who don't see things the way we see them. Where is the ravishing knowledge of God in our churches? It is a wonder that absconded the Church, and it is rarely found in many of our churches. There must be a desperate seeking of God in our hearts before we can experience the ravishing knowledge of God. There is a ravishing inward revelation of God that can be experienced within the deepest of our heart. Such inward revelation of God cannot be explained, only experienced.

How to Abide in Christ

If abide has such a profound effect in our relationship with God, and is the key to live a satisfying fruitful life, and is the only way to truly know God in personal experience; the natural question that should spring from our restless hearts should be, how do I abide in Christ? The answer comes in three ways:

i.   **Devoted Time for Prayer:** the word "Abide," implies to stay for the long run. Quick and rushed prayer will not suffice in abiding. We must set aside adequate time devoted to prayer, and jealousy guard it. We must also learn to wake up early in the morning to spend sufficient quality time with God; before our busy schedules take off. Whether we pray through verbal prayer, or talk to God only with our hearts, or simply listen to God, it matters not. The main point is that we spend adequate time in His presence, enough to build a stable and vital relationship with God. Waking up early in the morning may be a challenge, if you are not used to it; but if you are willing, and ask God for help, God will wake you up, and help you to pray and spend time with Him. If you don't give up, it will eventually become your second nature. Let your prayers be sincere and without pretense, and you are guaranteed God's presence. Prayer is not about feelings, but about an unwavering commitment to spend time with God. Those who pray the most, abide the most. And those who abide the most, will have more of the presence of God in their lives.

ii.   **Devoted Time for Bible Reading:** In prayer, we do most of the talking; in Bible reading, God does all the talking. Thus prayer and Bible reading creates a very balanced two-way communication with God, which is essential for us to have a healthy relationship with God. We must set aside adequate time devoted to Bible reading and jealously guard it. We must find our perfect quiet spot where we can read our Bible undisturbed. And daily meet there with God and attentively pay attention to what He has to say to us. If you read your Bible with a deep desire to hear from God, God will speak to your heart. And when you learn to cherish His written word, He will speak with a still small voice in the inmost inner chambers of your heart. It is disheartening, that many good Christians that love God, have never read the Bible from cover to cover. Therefore, their knowledge of God is mostly shaped and influenced by others' knowledge and experience of God. Second hand knowledge and experience of God will not suffice in abiding. We must know the Word of God for ourselves, before we can truly abide. If you have not done so, set aside ample time to read the Bible from Genesis to Revelation, that you may have an overall idea of what the Bible actually teaches. It will also help you to know how God speaks. It will teach you to recognize the voice of God, and distinguish God's voice from the voice of the flesh and the voice of the devil. You can start by deciding on how many chapters you want to read each day, and then by God's grace, try to stick to your daily reading goals. It would be wise to mix your readings, such as a few chapters from the Old Testament, coupled with a few Psalms, and a few chapters from New Testament. Bible reading is not about feelings, but about an untiring commitment to spend time with God. Those who read their Bible the most, abide the most. And those who abide the most, will have more of the knowledge of God manifested in and through their lives.

iii.   **Awareness of God:** The epitome of abiding, is the constant awareness of God's presence in our daily lives. There is absolutely no place where God is not. We do not need to climb the high mountains to find God. Wherever we are, God is right in front of us. He waits for us to awake out of our spiritual slumber and reach out to Him with the voice of our heart, and gaze upon Him with the eyes of our soul. We must always be aware that God is in front of us; whether we are conscious of it or not. As David says, *"I have set the Lord always before me"* (Psalm 16:8); and as Paul announced to Athenians, and in them, the whole human race, *"He [God] is not far from each one of us"* (Acts 17:27). In the beginning it may take much effort to set God before our eyes, and practice the awareness of the presence of God in our daily lives, but once the spiritual habit is formed, and the soul made acquainted with the presence of God, in time the soul will turn to God on its own accord. Now in order that we may live our lives in firm awareness of God's presence, we must:

a) **Keep a Non-stop Conversation with God:** This the apostle Paul calls, *"Praying without ceasing."* It is absolutely possible to maintain a non-stop conversation with God without affecting our daily duties in our respective workplaces. It doesn't matter where we are placed: office, car, shop, factory, restaurant, construction and others. We are not always busy; we all have brief times of release, and if we use that time to turn to God, we can maintain a never ending conversation between our souls and God. It is like excusing yourself from a visiting friend, for a phone call, then returning and resuming the conversation where you left off. The greatest calling and duty of our lives is our constant conversation with God. All our duties at home or workplace are intercepting phone calls that steal our attention from God for a while. But once our duty is done, we must return to the main thing — our conversation with God.

b) **Do All Things to the Glory of God:** The surest way to establish ourselves in the presence of God is to try to always do, say, and think everything to the glory of God. When we direct every act, word and thought towards God's glory, we maintain a constant awareness of God, every second of our lives.

c) **Seek God's Help and Guidance:** The reason why people that abide in Christ are so fruitful in their calling, is the gracious and instantaneous access to God's help and guidance they possess. Whatever our duty, low or high, small or great, insignificant or complex, we must never shy away from calling upon God to be with us. God is well pleased of our total dependence on Him.

d) **Fix our Eyes on God:** The primary focus of our lives should be God. Everything and everyone else, is a distraction and an intruder. We must always remember that, to be with God is to be absent from creation, and to be with creatures is to be absent from the Creator. Each one of us must choose our portion. The success of our abiding in Christ hinges on the choice of our focus. We choose Christ or people or things? The choice is absolutely ours. Whoever and whatever we make our daily focal point, that is the center of our lives, and ultimately the God of our life.

To abide in Christ is to gaze on Him with the eyes of our inner being; to lift up our heart to Him, acknowledge His all-pervading presence in our life, and follow the prompts of the Holy Spirit as the Spirit leads us. Right here, in walking daily the narrow way with our eyes fixed on Jesus our Lord, is where we ought to live all the days of our lives, Amen.

Lord, I want to follow You wholehearted, but my deceitful heart refuses to give up all its life-long plans and dreams. I want to be whole Yours but plans and dreams keep on pulling me from the narrow way. Please give me grace to surrender all my plans and dreams to You. And please be pleased to pluck from my heart, by the root, all my desires, dreams and plans that contradict and oppose Your perfect will for my life, in Jesus name I pray, Amen.

Meditation Time:

Scripture Reading: Morning: Revelation 14; Noon: Jeremiah 6; Evening: John 8.

Memory Precept: *"Thus says the LORD: 'Stand in the ways and see, and ask for the old paths, where the good way is, and walk in it; then you will find rest for your souls'"* (Jeremiah 6:16).

Memory Promise: *"Then Jesus spoke to them again, saying, 'I am the light of the world. He who follows Me shall not walk in darkness, but have the light of life"* (John 8:12).

And:
"And the LORD, He is the One who goes before you. He will be with you, He will not leave you nor forsake you; do not fear nor be dismayed" (Deuteronomy31:8).

Commitment to Obey the Precept & Having Faith on the Promise: God must lead me in everything, and by His enabling grace, I must faithfully follow as the Holy Spirit leads. No more leading myself. No more following my own plans and dreams. From this day forward, I consciously choose to give up the master plan of my life that keeps on taking me away from the will of God. I choose, by the grace of God, to let God's plan for my life lead my life. Whether I like it or not. I choose to trust that God will make all things work for my good. *"Your word is a lamp to my feet and a light to my path"* (Psalm 119:105).

Heart-talk: Pour your heart to God, be sincere and honest, tell Him how you really feel, not what you think is acceptable; just pour your heart without being superficial. (Use a different note page, if you need more space):

_____

_____

_____

_____

_____

_____

_____

_____

_____

_____

_____

_____

_____

_____

_____

_____

_____

_____

_____

_____

_____

Dear Reader,

Thank you for taking the time to read this book, I really appreciate it.

I hope you have been blessed, inspired, and encouraged. If you have any suggestions, comments, or questions regarding a character, the story, or anything concerning this book, or if you just want to say hi, you can reach me on my personal email: ramostalaya@gmail.com

Readers have the power to make or break a book through reviews. If you were touched and you've enjoyed this book, please consider leaving a review on Amazon and Goodreads, even if it's just a short testimony; it would make all the difference and would be very much appreciated.

If you would like to receive an email when Ramos's next book is released, please go to: http://eepurl.com/-Mbnz. You will only be contacted when a new book is released, your email address will never be shared, and you can unsubscribe at any time. Thank you for your support.

Available Titles

By Ramos Talaya

Soul Revival: A 40 Day Journey to the Feet of Christ

Soul Revival is a practical 40 days' devotional that helps Christians draw closer to Jesus Christ our Lord and be spiritually revived.

www.ingramcontent.com/pod-product-compliance
Lightning Source LLC
LaVergne TN
LVHW011352080426
835511LV00005B/260